Handbook of the Soul

Of Technologies of the Soul

Ken Evans

authorHOUSE®

AuthorHouse™ UK Ltd.
500 Avebury Boulevard
Central Milton Keynes, MK9 2BE
www.authorhouse.co.uk
Phone: 08001974150

First published by AuthorHouse 10/15/2009

ISBN: 978-1-4490-2636-3 (sc)

This book is printed on acid-free paper.

Introduction

THIS BOOK IS AIMED AT anyone who is interested in the idea of souls, especially their own. It is written to help readers to explore and play with ideas which will help them to understand how souls operate as the centre of the human sense of Being.

After teaching Psychology and Philosophy for quite some time, I moved into researching problems in Health and Social Care of Elderly people. I soon discovered from them that however confused they became as a result of their dementia, they still retained an essential part of themselves, which was usually ignored by their so-called Carers. I discovered that the inner core of each person was very different from their exterior, and I found that if I ignored the external appearances of old age or other physical differences, and concentrated on their inner life; the part of a person which for centuries almost every culture in the whole world has recognised and referred to as the Soul, I was able to `connect` with them.

The more I thought about this, the more connections I found I could make. But I also knew that modern psychology has ditched the idea of soul, so I looked at all the various ways that people are influenced by this vacant space created by the denial of the existence of soul. Each problem I came across led to a kind of diary entry, which eventually became a sizeable collection of pieces, all on various aspects of the soul.

I also thought about how I could avoid these ideas appearing as a kind of `new age` spiritualism, and also avoid being seen as bound by any particular religious or theological connections; not an easy task. I also wanted these ideas to be easy to understand, as well as demonstrating how anyone would be able to apply these ideas, and techniques; so the way it is written is to try to keep a balance between `everyday` and `professional` terminology, but still with enough amusing and interesting connections to keep the readers attention and interest.

I have kept the technical stuff to a minimum, but I still thought it important to trace some of the historical and philosophical ideas of the soul, especially as some of the things that people of the past understood about being human, are still relevant today. I have also used the medieval rhetorical device known as Via Negativa, the artful way of saying something positive about the soul by charting and annotating its demise and diminution.

When I came to put all of the pieces together, I decided to turn it into a big poem, similar to the way Dante in his `Divine Comedy`, a long poem about a man who investigated what happens to Souls when people die. Dante's poem follows them into Hell, the darkest and loneliest place imaginable, and up through Purgatory, a kind of cosmic therapy room, and finally to the pinnacle of bliss- Heaven. As you follow the cantos, you will be retracing something akin to Dante's journey.

Souls connect us to each other, and to their surroundings, and to their environment, and to all other creatures. This book explains how to make these `connections`, between your outer self and your inner core, and with your loved ones, and all others, your daily experiences, the immediate environment, the cosmos and eternity.

The technology of the Soul may also be read as an instruction manual for repairing a damaged or neglected soul, and in this sense it is a hand-book for the care of the soul.

The Flight Of The Soul

ONE HOT SUMMER during a philosophy lecture a dandelion puff-ball floated into the room through the open window.

I recall that it had been uncomfortably hot for several days, and the steady heat had produced a soporific atmosphere in the room, making it impossible to work, and even more difficult to concentrate on philosophy. The tedium was caused as much by the monotonous whir of the motorised lawn mower running back and forth over the croquet lawn, as by the soft monotone of our lecturer, the only other sounds was that of occasional visiting insects, and then unexpectedly everyone became aware of the arrival of the dandelion puff-ball.

Its arrival was a welcome if small distraction, briefly taking our minds off philosophy, as all heads turned to watch its lilting waltz-like movement, floating and hovering, describing small movements back and forth, seeming to have a sense of direction and suddenly changing its course. We were all following it for some time before our speaker spotted it, who then tried to dismiss its presence by continuing his lecture, but the circumstances were that it, the puff-ball, had robbed him of our attention.

By now the floating spectre of white fluff had shifted towards the front of the class, hovering in front of him. He eyed it scornfully then announced,
"That is how I imagine the Soul!"
And then he returned to his notes as if nothing had occurred.

This minute fragment of an occurrence, for some strange reason, became rooted in my memory, to recur again and again, perhaps for eternity. Yet I cannot remember even the slightest fragment of the lecture, or much else of that time; but only that mind- changing moment of that flight of the soul.

Mind, Imagination And Soul

Modern day psychology has much to tell us about visual perception, memory and learning, for example, but when it comes to what goes on in minds, imagination and souls; aspects of what we might describe as a person's `inner life`, it is found wanting. The reasons for this are complex and convoluted, but stated simply and to the point, the reason is that contemporary psychology tends towards reductive materialism, and lacks both the theoretical insights and language to even begin explaining anything of anyone's `inner-life`. This huge gap in the middle of this self-proclaimed science renders it redundant as a means of understanding anything of importance about being human. This might seem harsh criticism, but anyone who wishes to dip into the subject will quickly discover that whatever cannot be measured or conform to scientific experimentation, is excluded from the disciplines' remit. Quite simply, the mind, imagination, and soul, are beyond measurement, and either regarded as fictions or redefined as something else, for example, the mind becomes mind/brain,

Almost from the beginning of modern psychology, starting with Wilhelm Wundt in Germany there were shaping influences intended to integrate psychology with biology and the then new science of physiology. These shaping influences have almost achieved this integration in the form of so-called evolutionary psychology, a Darwinian influenced approach which attempts to explain the `human condition` in terms of both physical and psychological adaptation.

One of the consequences of this `merger`, which included celebrating Darwin's bicentenary, has been a re-invigorated psychological theorising on the evolution of human behaviour. On the downside, has been a gradual descent into petty squabbles with opponents of the evolutionists' viewpoint unfortunately, the silliness of attacks and counter-attacks, through provocative book-titles and churlish advertisements, rather than strengthening their case, diminishes it. Ironically this `squabble has strengthened the case of their opponents and has served to refresh the general public's interest in the so-called God –Debate. In other words the New Darwinists have shot themselves in their, other-wise perfectly adapted foot!

But this `squabble` is a side issue to my thesis of the endangered soul. But my initial criticism of the inadequacy of contemporary psychology stands; and is somewhat reinforced by the stringently reductionist scientism of evolutionary psychology, which unlike the practitioners of standard contemporary psychology, whose strategy is to wriggle out of addressing aspects of the human condition it cannot measure, the evolutionists choose to deal with these through ridicule, which again undermines their claims to scientific objectivity and detachment.

Mind

Anyone with the slightest interest in the Mind/ Brain problem will be aware that those engaged in its research would prefer to be mindless, not personally but professionally, for when they encounter what they acknowledge to be the "hard problem", their sense of scientific certitude leaks away. So when confronted with questions about mind, like those of previous generations who tried to `square the circle`, the only solution is to deny its existence, or to redefine it as in some way linked with the brain.

But their problem with minds is that they simply are not physical or material, and in this sense are similar to `ideas`, which no doubt like a joy-rider, ride the neural pathways, but are beyond the reach of physics. While we know it is possible to observe brain activity using electroencephalography and magneto encephalography, we also know that there is no analogous relationship between the indications of increased blood-flow and the actual content of the thought. The simple reason for this is that an `idea` is as invisible as the soul, or other abstractions such as `numbers`,

It seems that every generation of scientists, whatever their specialism is infused with, as part of their training, a doctrinal inclination to demolish and eradicate anything which is beyond their scientific grasp and control. And this imperative has recently become more aggressively ambitious with the `new Evolutionists, who under a banner of ``Consilience` they wish to subjugate all human knowledge under the one common heading of `Evolutionary Biology`. To make their case they use ingenious arguments and evidence, extrapolated from the size and shapes of fossilised skulls, from which they claim to read the `minds` of our ancestors, and speculate on the history of minds. The enthusiasm of the new evolutionary; biologists- physiologists- neuroscientists- psychologists- anthropologists has produced a torrent of publications, in which sadly, all of the fertile lushness of Darwin`s Galapagos, with its teeming life-forms, is somehow inoculated with a clinical impotence, in their anguished search for `hard` evidence, where there is only supposition. But as one of their prophets, Edward O Wilson admits, " I know that such reductivism is not popular outside the natural sciences`,…the focus of the natural sciences ,…is a search for a new synthesis. `That is the goal, variously, in studies of the origin of the universe, the history of climate, the functioning of cells, the assembly of ecosystems, and the physical basis of the mind."

Minds remains mysterious, and even its physical counterpart –the brain is far from being understood, but at least it is possible to physically examine this strange organ, not that this will give any clues to its internal capabilities, for despite its bland appearance, it is the seat of consciousness deceptively and secretly guarding secrets beyond discovery.

The trouble with mind is that it is something non material, issuing, emerging, coming out of something material, which interferes with any new evolutionary scientists` basic understanding of physics and the physical world, yet almost certainly they would willingly accept the reverse in quantum cosmological explanations, that not only minds, but the whole universe could have arisen as a *quantum fluctuation* out of nothing at all. In other words all the material of the universe, literally `becoming` , into exixtence physically and materialistically ex nihilo; understandably the assault on their sense of logic must be painfully overwhelming.

While there is general agreement that the mind cannot exist without the brain, there is no general agreement that they are the same thing, or even similar. The brain is a functioning part of the body, while the mind has access to other dimensions, to infinite intellectual landscapes and seascapes and which the brain, by comparison, occupies but a small and dull space.

Ken Evans

By the `Mind` we mean the vast territory we call the human condition and human experience, to be explored and opened-up using ideas as our maps. Places both metaphorical and actual, always shaped, even minimally, by human activity, where we spend much of our lives; places as small and intimate as Xavier de Maistre`s tiny `Room`, or as expansive and endless as Siberian wastelands, or as despairing as the dark interior of the Congo, distorted by the private greed and cruelty of ruthless Rulers, and besides these, places where we can meet other minds and gauge the boundaries of what it means to be ourselves.

We share our journeys with others through our time-and-space bound cultures, which we are able to transcend through our imagination- vehicles of our souls, using memories and myth and music, and stories that we conjure out of our fleeting thoughts and instances, traversing time and space, timelessly and from the comfort of anywhere we happen to be. This surely is Milan Kundera`s incredible lightness of being, grounded by the ballast of events we call history. Places, not only for us to bask in sweet moments of divine pleasures, but also to be shamefully and irresistibly fascinated by incidents of extreme acts of human cruelty; our curiosity condemning us in our vicarious shame!

I see and feel `The horror! The horror! ` of Conrad`s Kurtz in The Heart of Darkness, when I read accounts of terror, for example during the early colonisation of the Congo. How can we bear it? How can I express it, or sum it up in a few words, for in our minds, words become pictures. ?

"The baskets of severed hands set down at the feet of the European post commanders, which became the symbol of the Congo Free State. ... The collection of hands became an end in itself. Force Publique soldiers brought them to the stations in place of rubber; they even went out to harvest them instead of rubber... They became a sort of currency. They came to be used to make up for shortfalls in rubber quotas, to replace... the people who were demanded for the forced labour gangs; and the Force Publique soldiers were paid their bonuses on the basis of how many hands they collected."

The powerful people from whatever quarter ruled, and continue to rule their colonies by terror, they understood the necessity of invoking fear in the minds of those they wished to control, and they knew that terror is one of the cardinal points on every human map. Even at the domestic level, in the relations of two individuals, there is room for terror!

But other points of the human compass which rescue us from` the horror` also come as thoughts, sometimes playfully or at other times profoundly, whatever the case we frequently are caught unawares, surprised by our own inner resources. Then our mind becomes the playground of our thoughts, in reminiscing, we replay complete episodes as if hypnotised, we see and hear ourselves as if we are outside time, recapturing the joy and the delight, the fun, excitement, gravity, sadness. Like the reheated remains of a meal from yesterday, we savour different flavours, different sensations, the minutiae of memory; this is transcendence, for this is the realm of the senses inhabiting our minds.

And yet besides the territory of our own minds there is more, there are, as it were, huge continents of other minds, stretching to infinity, to which we can connect, and which, in some small ways, become extensions of our own imagination, reshaping our own internal landscape to the extent that we lose our sense of individuality, becoming inhabitants of a universal mind. From time to time we hear or read about something which registers with our mind, even possibly something quite obscure, but which resonates sufficiently to set our thoughts in action. The moment might pass, or it might return again and again, but for most of us we cannot tolerate for too long an unanswered question, we must accept that the mind is a hard task master.

When I heard about the eleventh century Chinese `Tale of Genji`, with its four hundred characters without names, whose lives seem to flow from one event to another without any real plot, I knew immediately that there was a place there for me. And the same also with Borges` Library of Babel`, a place that could certainly occupy a whole lifetime of anyone with a fondness for books , as it consisted of an endless expanse of interlocking hexagonal rooms, each room containing the basic furniture, and in each room, four walls of bookshelves. I imagine myself as one of the inhabitants of this amazing library, believing with the other inhabitants there that the books contain all wisdom, when in fact they contain only combinations of letters and spaces. But perhaps with the others there, I too would also be sure that this endless library must contain every book that has, or might be written, and with translations of every language which has ever existed, in multiple versions.

On reading about this library, in my mind I am already chatting, and sauntering from room to room with Borges in exactly the same way that he was able to thumb his way through some of the fifteen hundred, or so titles, real and imaginary which constituted Sir Thomas Browne's library. The 1711 *Sales Auction Catalogue of the Library of Sir Thomas Browne*, included the latest thoughts on; theology, history, geography philology, philosophy, anatomy, cartography, embryology, medicine, cosmography, ornithology, mineralogy, zoology, law, mathematics, geometry, astrology, chemistry, astrology, alchemy, physiology, travel. Browne could read and write in seven languages; French, Italian, Spanish, Dutch, Classical Greek and Hebrew, as well as the basic requirement for a scholar of that time, Latin. His own written work, especially; Pseudodoxia Epidemica, Hydriotophia-Urn Burial, and The Garden of Cyrus, read like gentle conversations with a patient and learned country doctor, who whilst pottering in his garden shed, is willing to share his thoughts with anyone who might show an interest.

In the mindfulness of Borges and Browne, their erudition becomes a conduit for ideas on which they leave their own mark before sharing them with others. Anyone who connects with, even just one of their ideas, becomes part of the `whole` as John Donne eloquently expresses in his Meditations;

"All mankind is of one author, and is one volume; when one man dies, one chapter is not torn out of the book, but translated into a better language; and every chapter must be so translated....No man is an Island, entire of itself; every man is a piece of the Continent, a part of the main".

The Mind's capability for interconnectedness is its unique transcendent purpose, operating cognitively and emotionally, it is also this aspect of mind, its capacity for interconnectedness which is the distinguishing feature which identifies it as uniquely different from its material counterpart the brain.

The human capacity to connect is also the basis of love in its broadest sense, not just in the romantic sense, but more generally in the ways we extend our concerns for others, for example in our shared sentiments of sympathy for people in disasters on the other side of the world. We connect with them in our thoughts, and assisting in their relief .

The sensation of this interconnectedness can be so overwhelming for some people that it amounts to extra-sensory perception. Their hunches and intuitions allow them to live `closely` with their loved ones. We know also that when we lose this `connectedness`, we have fallen out of love, or perhaps did not have it in the first place. In Ian McEwen's `On Chesil Beach`, a doomed couple , whilst imagining they are in love, failed to `connect` and reaped the direst consequences. And in `Howards End`, E.M.Forster`s epigraph for the novel is, `Only connect...`, in which Margaret, an idealist who marries Henry Wilcox, a pragmatic businessman, discovers the impossibility for love without connectedness.

"It did not seem so difficult. She need trouble him with no gift of her own. She would only point out the salvation that was latent in his own soul, and in the soul of everyman. Only connect! That was the whole of her sermon. Only connect the prose and the passion, and both will be exalted, and human love will be seen at its highest. Live in fragments no longer. Only connect, and the beast and the monk, robbed of isolation that is life to either, will die.

Nor was the message difficult to give. It need not take the form of a `good talking `. By quiet indications the bridge would be built and span their lives with beauty.

But she failed. For there was one quality in Henry for which she never prepared, however much she reminded herself of it: his obtuseness. He simply did not notice things, and there was no more to be said."

Forster's use of the adverb `only` in his pithy epigram `only connect`, in this instance meaning, *at the very least,* is tantalisingly simple, but in fact carries an enormous weight of several philosophies, or rather philosophical models underpinning many psychotherapeutic approaches, especially expressive therapies. These therapies focus on reintegrating `shattered` personalities and reconnecting personal relationships using a wide range of intervention techniques, but in one way or another, all forms of psychotherapy ultimately will focus on an individual's `self`, a straightforward concept in every-day terms, but a complex miasma in theoretical terms.

Imagination

Considering the central importance of imagination in our understanding of what it means to be human, we should expect an equivalent level of importance to be shown to it in psychological studies. Unfortunately this is not the case in contemporary mainstream academic psychology, but there has been a trickle of interest in `imagination` in recent evolutionary psychology studies, which consider `imagination` as an adaptation, providing survival benefits to the human species. Much of this is speculative, but at least it is an indication that human imagination is worthy of research.

My own view is that `imagination` is too central to human experience and too complex to be `packaged ` within the usual restricted framework of academic psychology, and that even to begin to investigate it would require a revolutionary re-examination of the epistemological paradigm of modern psychology. So we should not expect much of an explanation from that direction.

Searching for definitions of imagination will teach us only one thing, that most scientific attempts to define it ironically lack the kind of imagination to grab our attention and interest. (One writer sees it as "a dim version of perception".) Yet imagination is not lacking in those who research in these areas, rather it is the restrictions of a reductionist- scientific mindset which sets their stultifying tone. It is much easier to try to understand it by considering our own experiences, such as the times that imagination holds us in its thrall, possessing us unawares, so to speak, and seemingly always waiting to fill the smallest vacuum in our, so-called rational thinking. It seems obvious then, when we try to think about it, that our imagination is permanently active, filling in the gaps between one conscious thought and the next. So that whatever emerges verbally or otherwise is bound to be partly the result of our imagination.

But there are times when our imagination dominates out thought, even possesses us, in our wishful thinking, during our fantasising, in brief ecstatic moments, or whilst reminiscing. But for me, most precious of all, when my thoughts drift off during brief occasions when half awake and dawn is breaking, and my bedroom is slowly suffused with a magical kind of fragile light, then my imagination, comes sauntering or strolling rather than running, carrying me like a child in a mysterious reverie, blissfully rummaging through my earliest recollections.

I recognise then that there are many modes of imagining, and it would be easy to assume that the imagining experience is more or less similar for everyone within the same culture, but like other human activities there will surely be variations between us, even some which are socially or psychologically unacceptable, such as psychological disorders or drug induced states. But broadly speaking there is something like a common imagination, or a common core, which besides other aspects of modern life, makes the entertainment business possible. Films, videos, video games, music and fashion are designed to reflect a common or mass imagination, and almost certainly these industries have shaped and nurtured this mass imagination to create passive consumers. And even if this is the case, there are almost certainly other layers of each persons imagination which is distinctively, privately, and secretly theirs, and is what distinctively constitutes their `self`. One of Freud's explanations for the active imagination is that we humans persistently seek pleasure, and that if reality denies us gratification then we seek it in our imagination.

But we know from our own experience that `imagined pleasures` are not substitutes for physical pleasures, this might be the case with fantasies, but the kind of imagining I associate with reverie is something different altogether.

There is a particular story, already re-told so many times that it must have absorbed the effects of so many imaginations, that it is no longer possible to be certain about what is historically `factual`. (My inverted comma around the word factual is because I have enormous difficulty with so-called facts!) The story is known as L`Inconnue de la Seine, (the unknown woman of the Seine ) Or rather it is the core, of a brief story of an unidentified young woman, perhaps younger than twenty, whose body was pulled out of the river Seine at the Quai de Louvre in Paris sometime in the late 1880s. The girl`s face was apparently so beautiful, untouched by the tragedy of her presumed suicide, that a pathologist of the Paris morgue secretly made a plaster-cast of her face, which he later displayed on a wall in his pathology room, and which remained there for some time, until some time later, a mask-maker fell in love with the face, and asked to copy it.

Within a few years thousands of copies had been made, and the young woman's story so powerfully captured the popular imagination, that her death-mask became a novelty and a fashionable decorative art object among the wealthy and the poor alike, turning up in even the remotest villages throughout France, and carrying with it many versions of the myth of the `unknown woman` , the Ophelia of the Seine.

By 1900 an English fiction writer, Richard Le Gallienne, from Liverpool had heard of the story of the mask, and published a novella in which a young poet falls in love with the young woman behind the mask, but who is also aware of its hypnotic beauty, and tries to break the spell of the mask has on him, which he names ` le Silencieux`, by shutting himself away in an isolated cottage, meditating on the enigmatic beauty of the mask. For many hours at a time his obsessive wish is for the mask to open its eyes, which the mask finally does, and smilingly she also opens her mouth, releasing a death-head moth, as a kind of curse on his obsessive imagination.

The story of L`Inconnue de la Seine, and the mask continued to appeal to the popular imagination and became, perhaps the first modern cult object. Such is the power of imagination that everyone who owned a copy of the mask embellished the story to suite their own experiences. Newspapers occasionally printed letters from individuals who wished to contribute their personal stories of the unknown woman, many claimed to have known her, and some described her last moments before her death, but her identity remained a mystery.

For a brief few decades which straddled the nineteenth and twentieth centuries, the enigmatic face became a fertile icon of the human imagination. The German poet Rilke, fascinated by the story, imagined the thoughts of undertakers washing the body of an unknown woman for burial, and in his poem ` Washing the Corpse, he describes how;
"They washed her neck
And because they knew nothing of her fate,
They made one up together, washing all the while."

A host of other writers felt the compulsion to contribute to the story, each with their own version of why and how the girl had been moved to take her own life. The writer Maurice Blanchet suggested that the girl died in a moment of extreme happiness, mimicking in his imagination Bernini's sculpture of St Theresa in ecstasy in the Santo Maria della Vittoria in Rome, capturing a moment of ecstasy perhaps. And also the Author of Lolita, Vladimir Nabakov, and the avant- garde photographer Man Ray who celebrated the memory of the pale maiden`s mask in a series of surrealistic pictures.

Whatever connections writers and artists made between their own imagination and the unknown young woman, they had collectively touched the imagination of a whole generation, creating a shared sense of loss through the tragic story of youthful beauty and death, a powerful combination which grants a kind of immortality, and which continues to resonate in the imagination of anyone who hears or reads this story even today.

There is a kind of magic in this story, created and communicated by the human imagination which lies beyond the reach of psychological researchers, and which even if it were totally `fictitious`, is grounded in ordinary individual's experience, who through there own imaginations vicariously connect with the beautiful Ophelia of the Seine, as grieving parent, lover, or sibling.

Such stories also provide us with a kind of raw material, a sort of repository of images and ideas on which our own imaginations can feed, and which energises our souls, the final end- point of all sensations. Freud attempts to explain the pleasure derived from these experiences as originating in the childish world of make-believe, and continuing into adulthood as a tendency to fantasising, but in my view this diminishes the depth, profundity, subtlety and eloquence of a mature imagination. Perhaps Freud found it too difficult to unravel the complexity of the human imagination, and settled for an explanation contrived to fit in with his reality theory, and which explained very little..

An example Freud uses is a fictitious short story about a young archaeologist, Norbert Hanold, who fantasises about `a fully-grown girl` on a Roman `relief`, who he called `Gravida`-` the girl who steps along`. Norbert Hanold becomes so intrigued by the image of the girl, imagining that he can read the girl's biography into the image, and even dreams about her. In his dream he sees her, `stepping along` in Pompeii at the time of the eruption of Mount Vesuvius, and he shouts out a warning to her to take cover. But the girl appeared unperturbed, turned to look at him, and continued walking towards the portico of Apollo` Temple, where she lay down on the steps, and slowly turned to marble. After relating the story, Freud's own fertile imagination then goes to work to translate " Hanold`s dream as an erotic interlude, suggesting also that Hanold had a neurotic fear of relating to `real` women.

Other examples Freud uses when discussing imagination suggests that he had considerable difficulty drawing boundaries between supposedly `normal` imagination and neurotic delusions, which he treated as a form of mental illness. Considering this dilemma, it is puzzling that Freud, who could hardly have avoided acquaintance with the public interest in the story of L`Inconnue de la Seine, chose not to investigate the phenomenon of a public imagination, and the role of imagination, more generally, in ordinary situations in every-day life.

Within Freud's lifetime the public imagination became increasingly open to manipulation through the development of cheaply available fiction literature, through popular magazines carrying instalments of stories by Alexander Dumas in France, Charles Dickens in England, Edgar Allan Poe in America, and lesser known authors throughout Europe. This was also the time of the development of cinema, and a little later, of publicly transmitted television, all combining to expand access to a public imagination. For example in cinema, even in the earliest films the emphasis was on the imaginative depiction of every-day life, using special effects techniques, transforming what previously could only be imagined into believable visual displays. By the time Freud was in his mid fifties, every European country had its cinema-going public, talking about the latest release, and enjoying the new epics such as the Italian film –maker, Giovanni Patrtone`s two reel epic, "The Fall of Troy" (1912)

The availability of cheap mass produced fiction magazines, and a world-wide boom in cinema, and the arrival of public television transmission could not have passed Freud`s notice as dramatic evidence of these new fertile technologies of the imagination, yet he chose not to consider them as a means of investigating the imagination.

In literature, Dostoyevsky, Lewis Carroll, Shelley, Kafka, and James Joyce were engaging the imagination influenced by Symbolist art and literature, sometimes featuring passion and hidden longings, and certainly it would have been impossible for Freud not to have been familiar with the ideas of Rudolf Eucken, a fellow German intellectual, who in 1908 won the Nobel Prize for literature for his philosophical writings on the tension between the Inner and Outer "reality", and the role of human imagination. Yet it seems that all of this passed him by, and besides this, the social and academic circles in which he moved would have precluded him from having any casual contact with ordinary working class people, and which above all else, would have provided him with the richest source of how vital is the imagination at every level of society.

Most published material explicitly about imagination tends to present it as a socially privileged activity, as if somehow it is likely to be less active among other groups. If Freud was correct, then it would be more prominent among those unable to realise their wishes, than those who are able to purchase their desires. If by imagination we mean the ability to create alternative worlds, then those whose need to do this will be the most productive!

Documents from the 19th century Workhouses, from the borders of Britain's far flung Empire, from the First World War trenches, from the Mines and the Factories, from the Gulags and the Concentration Camps, from the earliest Sociological Studies of traditional communities, the voices of ordinary men and women, and children, speak of their survival and how their hope, which in their situations was all that could be imagined, and which saved them from despair, allowed them to carry on living. Perhaps it is this particular quality of the human imagination, more than any other, which truly characterises uniquely what it is.

If there were to be a saint of the imagination it would have to be Scheherazade, the legendary Persian story-teller of a Thousand and One Nights, with her stories of love, tragedy, comedy, burlesques, eroticism, cruelty, affection, and stories within stories with all the twists of real-life, of dreams and prophecies, in which the whole of destiny tests Scheherazade's power of imagination in her bid to survive the night and live another day.

True stories of survival, in sometimes impossible circumstances, might simply be due to fortunate circumstances, for example an earthquake victim might escape death because they just happen to be in the right place at the right time, and in this case they could hardly claim to have survived because of their ingenuity. But `survivors` of long-term extreme situations, such as hostages held by terrorists, or in rare and bizarre cases, young women imprisoned as sex slaves, who survive against the odds because of their imagination, they survive by thinking the impossible, and also by imagining themselves as survivors. Aleksandr Solzhenitsyn describes the oppression and the survival ethic of the Stalinist's Gulags, for example in his short novel, `One Day in the Life of Ivan Denisovich`,in which he describes how the whole camp lives by the rule of the survival of the fittest. The story details the small but incremental strategies for survival, such as accumulating small morsels of food, and trading them for favours. For the prisoners to satisfactorily survive another day was contentment, which the prisoners put down to luck, and not to their cleverness, but to them it amounted to the same thing, they had survived. At the end of one day, Ivan Denisovich Shukov went to sleep fully content. He'd had many strokes of luck that day.

Soul

Soul is less controversial than mind to the world of science, because irrefutably, it does not, and has not existed in the western world since the seventeenth century; or rather it has incrementally withered away as aggressive materialism progressively took hold in western civilisation. As secularisation advanced, the fate of the soul, which had for hundreds of years been monopolised by the institutionalised religions, became culturally marginalised, and eventually clinicised by the twin institutions of psychology and psychotherapy, leaving an emotional gap in how ordinary people felt about, understood and expressed their experience of an inner life.

The social sciences which underpin psychotherapy have attempted to replace the concept of soul with the less distinctive concept of `self`, which in one of its many popularised versions is a fragmented social construct, similar to Hume's `bundle theory of personality. Yet despite the secularising inclinations of modern society, the idea of soul survives in the cultural recesses of western society, mainly as a vague sense of an inner core of being. And while for the majority of us in western societies God has almost completely disappeared, the non denominational soul survives, almost but not totally detached from its religious connections.

So this modern semi-secularised soul is a diminished version of its pre-enlightenment essence, and is perhaps a scaled-down version of its Platonic original, but still in some way the central core of an individual's being, and still distinctively different from the hypothesised `self`.

The most compelling argument for the soul is its agency or volition, otherwise described by Schopenhauer as `Will`, that "is the innermost essence, the kernel, or every particular thing and also of the whole. It appears in every (apparently) blindly acting force of nature, and also in the deliberate conduct of man...." In other words soul as I understand it is the locus and the psychic centre of activity, initiating and concluding human thoughts, actions and activity, and it is the focal point of `being`. Physiology and psychology describe human actions in mechanical and machine-like terms, analogously, in which movements and muscles are activated by nerves similar to levers and pulleys; but both sciences fail to locate the `initiator`, the `something` that initiates the mechanical processes which cause our bodies to move and act.

Psychology describes the process as a series, beginning perhaps with *attention*-our contact with our environment, *perception*-our responses through our senses with our immediate environment, cognition- our mental responses, including prior experience drawn from our *memory* system, which finally activate nerves and muscles. As a simple description of how things work, this simple analogy of human motivation is perhaps sufficient as far as it goes, but it does not explain `intention`, the purposeful articulation of an idea or a wish or a desire! Certainly, desires are articulated by our souls.

In Aristotle's `De Anima` the soul is the source of motion, because humans and animals desire things and consequently, in order to satisfy these desires they acquire locomotion. But Aristotle points out that *desire* cannot account for all purposive movement towards achieving goals, because many of our bodily movements are automatic,(*fixed action patterns* in psychological terms). It is only when a desire, conceived within the soul, and activated by the *imagination*, and if sufficiently compulsive to overcome rationalised reservations, motivates body movements and actions. Freud`s description of the opposing forces of Id and Ego reflects similar theorising and explanations, an explanation which also corresponds to Plato`s (Phaedrus) metaphor of the Soul in its chariot powered by two horses, a dark horse of the *passions* and a white horse of *reason.*

Imagine for example a simple scenario such as a parent and a young child interacting, with its buzzing confusion of messages and signals back and forth between the two. Among the many signals from the child there is perhaps one, signalling the desire for an explicit display of affection from the parent, and among the complexity of these verbal and non-verbal signals, something triggers the desire in the soul of the parent to perhaps; reach out, to touch, to embrace, to hold, to kiss, to connect in some demonstrable way. In this brief moment the shared memories of parent and child momentarily fuse providing the frisson of the connectedness. And in one way or another, the soul of each is energised, enriched and replenished, or alternatively, there is movement in two bodies, but nothing mysteriously happens!

Disordered Occurances

I cannot mention its name, or even its location for it is still there; perhaps operating in more or less the same way as I remember. And when I think about that place I tremble to think of the despair of its inhabitants then and perhaps now.

To any stranger, perhaps out for a drive in the country or by chance having taken a wrong turning through those convoluted country roads, the place would appear to be what it once was, a Vicarage a late eighteenth century country residence, imposing and substantial, but now sadly showing signs of neglect, yet giving no indication of its present purpose of accommodating nearly one hundred elderly dementia sufferers.

There are no signboards, and only rare outside activity; it`s internal activity, like that of its inhabitants, is closed and shuttered from the rest of the world.

My own arrival at this place was the result of a series of events, starting with researching age-related health and social care problems, I had been working in a university psychology department, and moved to a local authority social services department to continue my research, which was mainly concerned with policies and procedures. At this point I had no formal contact with elderly people; most of what I did was book-based. One thing led to another, I visited hospitals and care homes for elderly people, and gradually became involved in writing reports on social care issues, and because of my psychology background, I was manoeuvred into taking responsibility for assessments. Finally I moved to work for a ` provider of social care for the elderly, owners of places accommodating EMI residents, those diagnosed as being `elderly mentally infirm`, an oddly antiquated description of people with age-related mental illnesses, mainly dementia in its several forms.

So by the time that I arrived for the first time at `the place`, I had already seen the insides of many similar establishments, each with its own refinements, but mainly all belonging to the same epoch, with similar names and similar atmosphere. But for all the others, from one end of the county to the other, I knew only as a visitor, as someone excluded from the manifestations of internal daily events. But now, as I recall on driving through the gates of the place and knocking on the main door of the house, I was earnestly searching for some indication of how I would fit in there. I really had no idea what to expect or what sense we (me and the residents) would make of each other!

Friedrich Nietzche, the German philosopher, whose extreme sanity eventually caused him to become mad, had a strange idea, the idea of eternal recurrence, an idea which once discovered becomes increasingly less strange, and returns me time and time again to the several occurrences at that, the interiority of the place, signifying for me the closed and battened –down interiority of its inhabitants.

My returns are always to the so-called Lounge, a vast sprawling extension to the back of the original house, overlooking the one-time croquet lawn- now gone to seed- which was the centre stage for most of the every-day occurrences, and where most of the residents spent most of their time. In this expanse of space there were clusters of arm-chairs, and coffee tables, and several televisions, and dinning tables, and in one corner, on a shelf , an empty fish aquarium , with no water and no fish, but the focus of attention of several frail looking residents, looking intently at the invisible fish.

As I was being shown round the Place I felt an unusual feeling of isolation. The faces of both residents and staff displaying a cold vacant impenetrable stare, a discomforting ghoulish blankness, which I would later discover was like drawn curtains to close off the outside world, and providing at least some small protection from the pain of the hopelessness of their isolation.

Each day I would drive the one hour journey to and from the Place, playing a mixture of music , the songs of Bob Dylan and my Classical favourites, but as time went on, it was always Mozart`s Requiem, which re-energised me and kept me sane, for my journey between my home and the Place came to resemble a kind of deep sea divers air lock, which allowed me to `normalise` between the different atmospheres.

For the first few weeks I liaised with external social services departments, but gradually I was pulled into dealing with small incidents which the staff assumed, I as a `psychologist`, had secret knowledge of techniques with which to pacify troubled minds. On one of these occasions I was asked to deal with an incident involving a remarkably small and frail woman, whose lilting body movements seemed to suggest that she was hypnotically under a dancing spell, and according to her Carers was having `one of her turns`. All I could gather quickly from the care staff was that there were occasions when this otherwise `quiet lady` would quite suddenly choose not to cooperate with the care staff, and would waltz around the lounge like a drunken boxer, dancing in and out of other resident's rooms, trashing their few personal treasures, and generally causing mayhem. Generally, it seemed, the care staff could handle it, but not this time. This time she had become so agitated by something, that she angrily pulled another 'docile' sleeping woman from her bed by her hair, and was on a trail of destruction, turning everything in her path upside down in her desperate search for her lost children.

Some of the care staff had taken cover behind a large door to avoid being attacked by the frenzied mother, calling her lost children and hurling abuse at anyone daring to intervene. As I arrived matters seemed to be getting worse, there was already a trail of debris, as she searched any room she was able to enter, and frenziedly rattling doors in her effort to locate her lost or hidden children.

I was aware of these occasional occurrences, and had witnessed these agitated moods before, and noticed that she usually ran out of steam, usually collapsing and then falling asleep, but on this occasion when I arrived on the scene, she had already been engaged in her search for more than four hours, and showed no signs of exhaustion. In fact there had been unsuccessful attempts to intervene and restrain her, which had made her even more determined that she would soon find her lost children.

As I approached, she was running between doors along one of the corridors, trying the door handles, and shaking them in desperation to escape, and desperately calling the names of her children. I held back, trying to give her space, but calling her name, she turned and looked at me, a mixture of expressions on her face; of fear and desperation, and for a while it seemed that she was weighing up the situation, her head lilting tantalisingly from side to side, and then suddenly she became still.

She moved her head, looking around as if locating a sound; I thought that perhaps this might have been one of Nietzsche's recurrences, and that part of her internal script which governed her behaviour was set to finish with the discovery of her children, that would produce some catharsis, but no. Nobody was moving, the barricaded staff were silent, and from another part of the building there was the muffled strains of a Vera Lynn war-time song. It was barely audible but she had picked up the music.

Slowly she seemed to unwind, letting go of whatever it was that had possessed her, releasing the body contortions, and returning her to this other world. She started to cry, trying to find the words of the song in her confused memory, and singing between the sobs of her now hardly audible crying.

When I tried to think of an explanation for this incidence it seemed possible that some terrible event had marked this poor woman's life, but later when I spoke to the staff about it, none of them had the slightest idea of her life or her background, confirming my guess that perhaps her sense of loss was real, and that her pain was beyond the reach of any in that place.

During the first few months of my time working at 'The Place', I had viewed the lounge as an inhospitable place, with its intentionally dim lighting and sparse furniture, and the residents scattered around in small groups, sometimes apparently enjoying each others company, but on closer observation, all disconnected from any shared sense of community or togetherness. In my recurrences I see it as the setting for a performance, which in essence it is. Its characters desolate, because their social circumstances have removed them to the margins of society, the same with their mental condition; their minds, imagination and their souls, also functioning as if on the margins, making it almost impossible for them to `connect`. I see them, nameless, like characters from the Chinese ` Tale of Genji`.

They are nameless because the protocols of confidentiality demands it, but also because although they are real people with real names that I remember, in any recurrence they become representative of all the others in similar circumstances, and similarly placed on the margins of society and sanity. Yet despite the supposed limitations, there were still desires and hopes and expectations.

For example, J, a seventy year old man, his recorded confabulations apparently masquerade, but containing threads of logical description about the a boat he claimed to be building, and his love affair with a `lady`, another resident. And G, a former automobile designer, who frequently showed me around 'The Place', insisting that he did not intend to sell it quite yet, and eloquently explaining everything cogently in his Oxbridge accent; and A the ship-yard welder, always being reprimanded by G for his lateness; and the many others, whose personas would repetitively emphasise that there is still enough Mind,

Imagination and Soul, with which to `connect`, and pull them back into the circle we dub humanity.

But sadly they are isolated by a `model of care` which medicates and stabilises them, and maintains their position in the status quo. But amazingly there were one or two of them, who perhaps by mere chance, managed to escape the inevitable extinction of that Place.

I never went into any of the residents' rooms in any of the Care Homes, but one morning I was asked to accompany the MD who was visiting another of the companies Homes. He was rushing through corridors, mid –morning, while staff were busily changing bed linen, and assisting residents to dress. He was in a great hurry and almost running past residents rooms, and I was trying to keep up with him, when I heard a pitiful cry for help from one of the rooms. I had also been running, but I stopped, or should I put it another way, I was stopped, by the desperate cry for help, and the desperate imploring expression on the grey face of a woman, her knees hunched up like a child's under the bed clothes, and her pleading gesture. I knew instinctively that I had to stop, and go into her room and help her.

She told me that she had lost one of her new slippers, and explained that it was somewhere, but that she couldn't find it, and that her daughter had gone to great trouble to choose and buy her new slippers, and now she has lost one of them, and her daughter would be upset about it. Her concern was not for the slipper as much as the thought of her daughter's distress. For the next few minutes I forgot that I should be accompanying my boss, and followed her instructions. I searched under the bed, in her wardrobe, behind the door, and anywhere she suggested the slipper might be, but I could not find it. Then amazingly for me, as I stood by her bed she looked at me, directly penetrating my defences. It was like looking into the face of Dorian Grey, for a brief moment her wrinkled face seemed to shed its years, and my thoughts were, that perhaps she had not lost her slipper, but that she was trying to communicate something much more important, something much deeper, that her life had been an eternal recurrence of loss, expressed now through her loss of a slipper. More surprising for me was the thought that it had not been me, but she who had reached out and to stop me in full flight, for no other reason than to `only connect`.

My daily journey to and from the Place was a daily interregnum, each morning on my way to work I would review some of the events from the previous day, and try and work out how I might be able to ease some of the confusion and pain of the Residents, and on the homeward journey, I would try and re-adjust to the outside world. But sometimes I would arrive home `heavily laden` with the many fragments of unresolverable occurrences still in my thoughts.

A particularly perplexing occurrence concerned Maria, an amiable Greek woman who seemed isolated and alone, always when ever I saw her sitting in the same place in the Lounge, usually smiling, and sometimes apparently singing to herself. She was plump and jolly-looking, always wearing a traditional black dress typical of elderly Greek ladies, with long grey hair coiled up in braids. When ever I passed her by and greeted her, she would mutter something in her own language, which led me to enquire if she was able to understand English. The general consensus was that she could understand, but chose not to speak it. My impression was that she seemed contented enough to sit alone, perhaps reliving her life in what memories remained, but one morning she was not where she usually sat. I was busy with several other residents, and did not discover until late in the afternoon, that Maria had not out of her room for several days, and that she had also not eaten any meals for three days.

When I asked the manager of the Place what was happening with Maria, I was told that Maria had turned her back on the world and probably had decided to die. This blandly delivered explanation alarmed me, and I drove home that afternoon with several gloomy scenarios circulating my imagination, and wondering why nobody had tried to reach out to connect with Maria.

The following morning I had decided that Maria deserved more than just a quiet acknowledgement of an apparent decision to die; I spoke to the manager again, and eventually was invited to view Maria in her room. Her single bed was positioned alongside the wall opposite to the door, and she was lying with her back to anyone entering, and I could see how this could be read as her turning away from the world. The Care Assistant with me called her name but there was no response, and I also tried to speak to her, but again there was nothing. Apparently she had not spoken or eaten, but had used the toilet while she was alone.

I raised the matter again with the manager, and asked if Maria had any family nearby, and if they had been contacted about her situation. I was alarmed by the response! Seemingly Maria really was alone, there were distant family members but a long way away, who rarely visited, and according to the manager, were not very interested in Maria's life.

The gloomy scenarios continued to play in my mind, and I started to think about Maria's final days, and what else I might be able to do to disallow a lonely death. I had noticed a crucifix on her bedside table, and reasoned that as she was Greek, that she might have been a practising catholic or Greek Orthodox adherent . I approached the manager again, and suggested that Maria might appreciate a visit from a priest. I had in mind that at least Maria would benefit in some way is she received a final blessing, but I did`nt share this idea with the manager, especially as she seemed to suggest that to bring in a priest was perhaps a waste of time. I knew that she was busy, so I suggested that I would arrange it, with her permission, which she agreed to somewhat reluctantly.

I spent the afternoon telephoning Catholic churches in and around the area, having to repeat my story each time I spoke to anyone, but finally one considerate priest advised me to telephone a Greek Orthodox priest, who was living several hours away by train, and that he might also be too busy or unable to make the long journey.

When I called him, I was not sure how I would be able to convey my conviction that a visit from him would perhaps be the last kind act from one human being to another for this very lonely soul. But somehow he caught the sense of my desperation, and promised to come to the place the following morning; I told the manager but she shrugged her shoulders, conveying a mild acquiescence.

The priest arrived just before lunchtime; when almost everybody was too busy to notice him. He was wearing a dark blue cassock, was bearded and was also wearing a traditional Greek Orthodox hat. Sitting in the office, we chatted about Maria, and about his church in Cyprus, and then asked if he could administer to Maria alone; I took him to her room, and left him there, and returned to the office, wondering what would happen next if she finally let go of her life, and who would arrange her funeral.

The manager came in with her sandwiches, and casually asked if the priest had arrived, when suddenly one of the Care staff arrived at the office to announce that Maria had appeared in the lounge demanding her lunch. Then the priest came back into the office and sat down. I could see immediately that the manager was dumbstruck, partly because of the news of Maria`s sudden resurrection, but also because of the priests strange presence; she clearly had no idea how to handle the situation and seemed somewhat shy of the strangeness of the slightly exotically dressed cleric. I sensed her inadequacy to connect to this stranger,and I could also see that the priest was also aware of this, so I briefly introduced them, and then asked what had happened to make Maria change her mind about leaving this world.

I can see him now, in that instance in time, sitting composed as if about to dispense to both of us, to the manager and to myself, a kind of grace. He sat upright and speaking gently with a conviction that he already knew the mind of Maria. He described how he had greeted her, and had begun reciting the prayers for departing souls, and how she had responded immediately to him when he asked her if she was ready to die. They had shared some prayers together, and she then declared how hungry she had been.

It was part of the manager's routine to hurriedly eat her lunch and return to her duties as soon as she was finished, but as the priest revealed some of experiences in tending the dying, she became transfixed, and continued to ask him how and why he knew about these things. The clumsiness of her language indicated a religious naivety, but also a growing fascination in what she was hearing, she quite obviously was smitten by his presence. He talked plainly and matter-of-factly about the soul, and she responded as if she also acknowledged its existence and its importance, and finally he had to say that he must go.

I accompanied him to his taxi, again thanking him and forcing on him his train fare, and returned to the office. The manager was still sitting there, and after a few minutes silence she said that she had been overcome by the priest's calmness and quiet dignity. She also unloaded her feelings about religion, and its hypocrisy and how meaningless it all was as far as she was concerned, but because of this priest, she had felt moved to the point of agreeing with me that perhaps the priest's prayers had somehow succeeded with Maria whereas everything and everyone else had failed to connect.

Life

The idea that mankind is Homo-Duplex re-emerges from time to time in new guises; as body and soul, negative and positive, with ` life` described scientifically or poetically, and so on. But there is more than just a small difference between a scientific and a non-scientific definition of Life. Life to a scientist is composed of lists of names of species and descriptions of chemical and electrical processes, while to us who merely posses it, we bumble in our attempts to say what we think it is. For whatever sense we can make of it to ourselves, we struggle to tell others how it really is for us. Even in the telling, and re-telling of our own versions to ourselves, unknown characters emerge which resemble us, but are not us, for it seems that we have as many lives as we have witnesses. It seems strange that the one subject we should know inside-out, when it comes to telling about it, it somehow eludes us.

It eludes us at deeper levels because the flow of consciousness is too complex and varied, our thoughts like star-bursts resisting the stasis of interpretation. By the time a particular thought has grabbed our attention, we have let go of others. What we hold is reduced to what we can make sense of, like a patchwork quilt with pieces missing. . And when we examine it, we know that what we hold, our view of our own life, is idiosyncratic. And that most of the time we are unsure where most of these thoughts come from, or what they mean and how they are linked to the things we do, or why we do the things that we do, or think the thoughts that seem to come to us unbidden.

This process of personal reflection continues to be debated by `specialists` such as psychologists, philosophers and psychotherapists, but there is considerable disagreement between the various explanations of how ordinary people understand and make sense of their lives. One suggestion is that through our imaginations we construct stories about our experiences of life by collecting *fragments* which we trim and shape and which approximates to reality! This idea is one of many *constructionist* theories, all pointing to the difficulties in introspection.

But besides the actual thinking involved in this kind of activity there is also the difficulty with the everyday use of language. To capture the complex and subtle nuances of these kinds of thoughts requires language skills equal to the sophistication of the thinking, and besides this, some of the personal impressions might not be explicable in mere words, but might occur musically or visually, and so they lie beyond normal language. In these times of diminishing language skills the possibility of capturing even a glimpse of our *essence* is greatly reduced, and for the majority of individuals, it is easier to reach out to ready-made approximations that flow continuously through audio/visual media of film and television, or not bother at all. Social commentators have noted the increasing extent to which Joe-public lives his life vicariously, even to the point of borrowing ready-made aphoristic statements which apparently sums-up his life, which he endorses by repeating as if they are his own thoughts. The extent to which individuals unwittingly absorb cultural stock phrases and re-present them as their own personal thoughts is an aspect of social development waiting to be researched!

Perhaps the most obvious conclusions we can draw from `our ringside seat of the modern culture show` is that for the majority of individuals, who have become totally homogenised to the extent that their sense of uniqueness has disappeared; personal reflection has become a redundant activity. The all pervasive mass media that inhabits even their living room in the form of an all-knowing oracle permits them to absorb information about everything except themselves. One of the consequences of this is that the idea of an authentic interior life has been marginalised, and become a peripheral concern and interest of a small minority of people. For them there is still the solace of contact with the deeper roots of their culture, through literature, and poetry and philosophy, and still the possibility of belief in a distinctive essence which underscores their sense of self. For them, they will wrestle with their thoughts and feelings about their daily lives and what sense they can make of it. Certainly they will share these thoughts with other like-minded others, and they will home-in to where there is food for these kinds of thoughts.

Samuel Beckett, whose whole body of published writing could be described as an experiment in this kind of thinking, wrote near the end of his life, at the age of seventy-six, "With diminished concentration, loss of memory, obscured intelligence...the more chance there is for saying something closest to what one really is. Even though everything seems inexpressible, there remains the need to express." To read any of Beckett`s plays is to be confronted by the profoundest elemental reflections and expressions of `the making sense of life`. In his prose-poem`Malone Dies` the apparently mundane recollections of a very old man transcend their common-place utterances, the plain words obscuring the depth and complexity of an awareness of "being" and living, and re-living and reassuring himself, and us his readers, that life has some meaning

Beckett`s brilliance lies not just in his remarkable grasp of language, but in his ability to capture the multi-dimensional images and meanings in a simple utterance, as Malone lies in his bed waiting to die ! For example at the beginning of his recollections of his `life`, Malone shares with us his private thoughts.

"This time I know where I am going, it is no longer the ancient night, the recent night. Now it is a game, I am going to play. I never knew how to play, till now. I longed to, but I knew it was impossible. And yet I often tried. I turned on all the lights, I took a good look all round, I began to play with what I saw. People and things ask nothing better than to play, certain animals too."

The rest of his death-bed soliloquy is a tantalising jumble of memories, recollections, stories, anecdotes, and insights, visions even! Telling the story of Macmann;

"One day, much later, to judge by his appearance, Macmann came to again, once again, in a kind of asylum. At first he did not know it was one, being plunged within it, but he was told so as soon as he was in a condition to receive the news. They said, in substance, You are now in the House of Saint John of God, with the number one hundred and sixty-six. Fear nothing, you are among friends. Friends; Well well. Take no thought for anything, it is we shall think and act for you now forward."

This apparent simple explanation of Macmann`s arrival in a mad house turns out to be a Dante-esque description of his arrival in heaven.

"Macmann did not immediately grasp that he was being spoken to. The room, or cell, in which he lay, was thronged with men and women dressed in white. They swarmed about his bed, those in the rear rising on tiptoe and craning their necks to get a better view of him. The speaker was a man, naturally, in the flower and prime of life, his features stamped with mildness and severity in equal proportions, and he wore a scraggy beard no doubt intended to heighten his resemblance to the Messsiah......
He finally handed this paper to Macmann, together with the stump of an indelible pencil, they point of which he first wetted with his lips, and requested him to sign, adding that it was a mere formality......Then, suddenly turning, he cried, What in God`s name are you all pushing for for Christ sake? And indeed the room was filling more and more, under the influx of fresh spectators."

In Malone's recollections, time and space become fluid, past present and future condense into now, the distinctions between real events and suppositions evaporate. His own personal experiences and those of others become elements of a common experience, for perhaps all human beings, trivial yet mythic archetypal visions of heaven metamorphose into images of the mad-house, life`s sublimest complexities are submerged in these deceptively simple descriptions. It seems that only at the time of "the dying of the light", almost when it is too late for reflection and evaluation, are we as individuals are able to say, how life has been!

The inscription; `Know Thyself` in the pronaos of the Temple of Apollo at Delphi, attributed to several ancient Greek sages sets us the impossible task of knowing who we really are and what meaning we give to our life. But it is even more demanding than asking who we are in an everyday sense, it directs us to seek a deeper knowledge of our inner core, penetrating the deeper layers of self, through a personal spiritual transformation and confronting our souls.

In asking who we are we begin by eliminating what we are not, and seeking the distinction between me and not me. This is the basic technology of the soul, for in seeking the basis of the ground of our being, the character of the soul we must identify and contemplate the essential interaction between the soul and some other elements, and psychic forces outside of it. What we discover is that in the course of this interaction, nothing is imbibed or consumed by the soul; rather it is motivated as if by induction or sympathetic movement, its energy generated entirely within itself. Our physical experience is similarly a harmonisation of an activated and excited soul.

How else can we put these ideas into words?

The Diminution Of The Soul

In everyday terms it is a strange idea that human progress might have already reached beyond modernisation to the post-modern condition, as if we have already surpassed the future. Meanwhile the triumph of commercialism in real terms exemplifies the implosion of values that characterises postmodernism. Although from time to time a new idea is floated which suggests that, in Western terms, the human spirit has not been completely extinguished, those who are seriously concerned about such matters await some expected critical moment, which they believe will usher in the final debate; some consequential event which will stand against the combined forces of materialism, capitalism and commercialism

What they really await is a miracle. Perhaps, from out of the crowd a small voice will declare that materialism, like the emperors new clothes, is naked, an idea based on a fiction, a capitalistic trick, and that what is required is a new metaphysic. This does not mean a thesis refuting the former metaphysics, but some ideas refining and re-defining in everyday language, what we mean by being human beyond the merely physical descriptions permitted by materialism. But this is no simple wish; in fact it is

Ken Evans

perhaps too sophisticated for a society already tamed by commercialism to visualise just how such ideas might engage the soporific numbed culture of late capitalism.. Its ramifications are that it would require an intellectual revolution; capable of re-evaluating fundamental ideas we have about ourselves, and our relationships with each other, about our understanding and beliefs about humanity, and human purpose, and a re-examination of intuition and introspection.

Perhaps such a revolution is not beyond possibility, but the debate cannot be restricted within the province of science, even if those who are its representatives insist that the only acceptable proof must operate within the canon of verifiability. Or even exclusively within any specific intellectual framework defined as philosophy, or the social sciences, or any privileged discourse, which is beyond common understanding. Although its working concepts might be intellectual products drawn from these sources, their application needs to be grounded in a language accessible to everyone.

One of the contradictions of materialism is that its products often embody anti-materialist concepts. Examples of this are to be found in the materials of pop culture; television programmes, videos, recorded music, clothes and dress accessories, etc., which provide a temporary escape from one kind of reality through alternative virtual realities through fantasy games and highly contrived so-called talent contests, by which mere mortals become briefly celebrity deities. It seems that the manufacturers and distributors of these fantasy products are unaware that the products themselves carry within them the seeds of their own destruction, and even the destruction of the entire capitalistic enterprise. Because it is through the use of fantasy, drawing on a vast reservoir of cultural ideas and images resonating other strands of meaning, which might occasionally, at an individual and personal level, stimulate unrealised sentiments and feelings, and a yearning for something with more depth. And when this happens it has the possibility of becoming for a brief moment, both the means of enlightenment and a personal crisis, which in most cases will be quickly relinquished because the effort to escape the mundane is too demanding in time and resources. But if and when this `moment of truth ` is experienced, it might have the startling effect of being something sublime, an epiphany, or as a distant hope of resolution.

To describe this `distant hope of resolution` as an `ache` might be nearer the truth, for individuals even in their most mundane conversations from time to time, touch on the subject of their own existence, especially at moments of despair, or when they are desperately hurt through loss or insult, or when sensing feelings of helplessness and hopelessness. To be present with others when this occurs is to be challenged by a similar kind of numbness, a spontaneous inability to respond appropriately. We think we should be able to understand, to comprehend because the other's despair is part of the human condition, and that in some way they must be like us, and because of this we believe that we should be able to intuitively grasp another's pain. We mistakenly assume that all pain is the same, except when we ourselves experience it. Then the complexity of pain stands as a perfect metaphor for the post-modernist human condition experienced both socially and individually as an implosion of meaning, the ultimate crisis of human identity.

It is at these points of the further reaches of human experience, as both Freud and Maslow describes them, that we are confronted by questions about ourselves. About who we are and our relationship with others, especially those others we love the most, not only those closest to us, but all of the others we share space with during our everyday activities. What might have been reasonably clear ideas to us, when trying to make sense of such moments becomes fuzzy, and indistinct? We become overwhelmed by the need to clarify things, to define, and to reconfirm who we are, and who we love. We have in our minds a straightforward account of these things, but through responding to our own `ache`, our distant hope of resolution of these questions, that we fabricate and reconstruct our relationships as we wish they might be.

We think, we feel, we hope that they are wholesome, at least for much of the time, and our mind returns to ourselves, and how others experience us, and what it is about ourselves that might be lovable, identifying that `something` that is beyond the merely physical, something we might describe as essentially me, my essence, my soul.

Western Culture

It is an open question to what extent any citizen understands the roots of their culture; perhaps for the majority of people they come and go, accepting things as they are, and raising few questions that will affect anyone beyond their immediate family. Yet for the majority of us, when we read or hear in the news media a reference to Western culture, we vaguely imagine a way of life that is defined by the differences of other cultures, defined mainly by the things we have which are different from the things that others have, or in most cases do not have. We in the west define ourselves by what we possess.

For those of us who might be intrigued by theses matters, they will already have scratched away at some of the ideas that have formed our ways of doing things. But for the majority, who intuitively know the impossible size of the task of identifying that crucial element that characterises our culture, and in the main content themselves with a surface reading of who we are as Westerners, and what Western culture might be about. For that majority, their understanding of their cultural roots is lodged in the historical minutiae of historical individuals or events, rather than the search for the soul of their nation, race or culture. Even for the most resistant school child, we learn at an early age that our most cherished values originated in other cultures, absorbed from elsewhere, and we are persuaded that our culture consists in layers, each one somehow contributing to the whole, but from there on all is mysterious and perhaps meaningless. But we carry on wondering about ourselves and about each other without really understanding the connection between culture and self.

Cultural theorists attempt to identify social processes, mechanisms and forces constituting the underlying dynamics of cultures, rather than examining the contributing layers from which the culture is composed, and which are more correctly the raw material of historical, sociological and anthropological analysis. Instead cultural theorists wish to identify the core assumptions, the beliefs, hopes and dreams which are embedded in the cultural myths, in the `conscience collective` so to speak, and which would reveal the psychological `pulse` of a people. Their quest is to dig deeper, and to lay bare the soul and its origin of a family of cultures, and to include those who claim affiliation, which in this case with the western world, and which already has been most notably laid bare by Friedrich Nietzsche in his `The Birth of Tragedy`.

Nietzsche's exposition of Western Culture has penetrated deeper than any other conventionally academic work, deeper than any vaguely comparable historical, philosophical or social analysis. Because his approach is not that of a conventional investigator, but rather that of a Shaman, and as a cultural shaman, he has summoned the spirits of our deepest cultural memories through the means of something more akin to divination, plunging his hands into the entrails of our fallen gods, and reading the character of our ancestral tribes. Our origin, he shows, lies in the irresolvable tension between Apollo and Dionysius, a tension between control and ecstasy; between intellectual detachment and raw flesh. For anyone who lives within the boundaries of western culture and who has failed to grasp this elemental characteristic of what drives them will misunderstand most of their own behaviour, their motivation, emotions and rationality. And more importantly they will also fail to understand their lives and the lives of others. Certainly it is possible to attempt to read cultures without getting blood on your hands, and without exposing yourself to the threat of spirit possession. But for Nietzsche, it was necessary to touch and smell the viscera of Western culture to be able to read it in the way that he did, and in gaining his privileged insights, paying the ultimate price for disembowelling the gods.

The essential message to the modern Western world is that in slaying the gods we have cut ourselves off from some, perhaps most, of the vital creative forces that held us in balance between joy and despair. We have sacrificed the dangerously ambiguous poetic for a safer, but enfeebled scientific certainty, and have come to value the predictably routine and concrete over abstraction and enchantment, seeking gold over love, and opting for the bland territory of the obvious against the possibility of paradise. These have become our preferences when we try to tell others who we are, and these are the real causes of our distress, and the virus in our souls.

Still Dancing To The Music

One of the difficulties, and perhaps it is the main difficulty, in discussing any aspect of life, of ordinary life that is as it is lived in an everyday sense, is that whatever our experiences, we describe and define these in physical terms, separating them from so-called fictional events because our functioning paradigm recognises only the physical and the material as real, and anything beyond this as either imaginary or belonging to the newly invented category of `virtual reality`. This way of thinking, or mode of thought is commonly assumed to be the prime characteristic of modernity, as evidence of being more advanced and more penetrating than previous epistemologies, mainly because this way of thinking is perceived to be more objective and more scientific.

There are several problems with this particular viewpoint, not least that to hold such a view that reality is limited to only the physical and material, is to shut off large areas of human experience as being without meaning and consequence. This implies that as part of the current paradigm, there is an inherent value system which states that there is only one kind of reality, and that for all those who think differently, those of other cultures, and all those of previous generations, `reality` is and was beyond their reach. And that within our own culture, for any individuals who hold views about multiple realities; by definition they must be mad. In fact it is a fundamental assumption of all modern theories of mental illness that being out of touch with this kind of reality is the central indicator of disordered thinking, and the root of mental illness, madness or psychological distress.

It is for these reasons that we are often reluctant to reflect too deeply on our own unusual thoughts and feelings, even privately. Because, although at one level of thinking we are able to dismiss some thoughts as aberrations, as quirky personal amusements, at another level we are frightened that these thoughts might carry us over the edge and into some hypothetical abyss. And also that once we have entered that territory, we would lose our grip on reality, and place ourselves outside the mainstream of rational life. For most of us and for most of the time we operate within the reassuringly safe paradigm of a tangibly- real physical reality, hurriedly dismissing irrational thoughts as peripheral, but sometimes not without experiencing the briefest frisson of combined terror and fascination, perhaps brief moments of madness, blending danger and ecstasy and moments of clarity and fulfilment.

And yet we seek this `madness` in literature, and drama, and music, and cinema, nurturing ourselves by externalising it, by trapping it within a physical container which allows us to turn it off should it begin to take hold, protecting ourselves against the possibility of it flowing inwards, panicking at the first signs of a take over, and fearing its power to possess us. Some authors identify this as a kind of psychic chaos, but in fact it has its own order and its own logic, and is far from being irrational in any sense of meaning; rather it constitutes a much older and fundamental vital force, more basic even than the kind of energy depicted as ID by Freud , for this is the raw energy of existence, the very essence of life itself, this is the Dionysian vitality which ultimately drives the universe. It is also the deep resonant note that sounded in Conrad`s Heart of Darkness, which we intuitively try to grasp in our most fundamental beliefs, and deepest thoughts about ourselves. But it is scary, very scary, and the whole of modern technology seems to have been invented to hold it at bay, to protect us from its power. And it is only by an act of will that we dismiss it from our modern goings on, but by some peculiar contradiction, in this very act of its denial we most readily submit to its power. For it lies hidden, at the root of our most modern technologies as the archetypal desire to refuse its control.

Its earliest manifestation is in the form of a dancing figure with deer head or mask, on the wall of a cave in Trois Freres in France, an image as old as the earliest humans, and still active as shaman in the wastelands of Siberia. And when these elemental forces were formalised by the Greeks, they became gods, transfigured through our need to communicate, providing further opportunities for negotiating in matters of life and death, by absorbing some of its energy in the healing temples as priests disguised as gods, curing patients by touch and words and music, with all the power of a modern placebo.

And just when we thought it was safe to come out of our temples, it wells up again in its ancient demand to which we still must obey.

Canto 1

WHO AND WHAT we are is fundamental to everything else we do, for not to have some idea of ourselves is the critical test of sanity, indeed of existence and being. Yet strangely, this is a matter of least concern for the majority of people. For most of us it is taken for granted that we simply `are`, and that speculation about `being` and associated issues are best left to philosophers and other specialists. It might also be an assumption that such matters are safe in their hands, and that they are able to define for us what it is to be human. If that is the case then we are mistaken, for definitions that value who and what we are, as persons, have been steadily diminishing over the last two centuries and now at the start of the twenty first century, have almost completely been eliminated.

The causes and reasons for this are complex, but for anyone interested in these issues, the difficult problem is in negotiating the gap between theorising with all of its convolutions, and the practical requirements of assisting ordinary people when these fundamental questions might be raised. A brief answer might be that the world has changed, and that our species, at one time central to the whole cosmos, has been relocated as one species among many, at one end of the evolutionary spectrum. But it is far more complicated than that, and the consequences are more serious than simply changing cosmologies, because who and what we are, affects how we treat one another, and ultimately how we feel and think about ourselves. And this in turn sets the agenda for all the myriad interactions that combine to underpin social life.

This is not a matter of concern at the mundane level, for in ordinary everyday conversations we continuously test ideas about ourselves and seek reassurance. But in extraordinary circumstances, the questioning might dig deeper and activate different levels of discourse. It is at these points that ordinary language fails, and that we discover the poverty of our current vocabulary and terminology to express our deeper feelings about ourselves. And if language shapes our thinking, as some psychological theories suggest, then it is necessary to examine the forces and influences that have reshaped human consciousness to understand why a void at this level of human interaction has become the tolerated norm.

Whenever issues concerning changes in consciousness are discussed, a small number of key points of reference are identified, including; the Enlightenment, Darwin's theory of Evolution, Freud's Personality theories, perhaps Weber's ominous warning of Disenchantment, and more recently the bundle of new sciences which include genetics and neurology. Their influence is set against a cultural and intellectual historical background, beginning at the end of the nineteenth century, with its response to burgeoning mass society, giving rise to massive and massing processes; including, mass production, mass consumption, mass media, mass destruction, mass murder in the form of genocide, and so on. Consequently the scale of human history expanded to gargantuan levels, diminishing by comparison, the meaning of individual person's lives. In all of this it has been impossible for individuals to try to make sense of the impact of these processes on personal relationships, or to understand how changes in personal values and manners have impacted on ordinary everyday relations. To try for an explanation at a very general level we only have to look around us, for examples of what might be described as, objectification of human relations, which are freely evident even in the most casual of human interactions. In fact even at such minimal levels of personal exchanges as purchasing a newspaper from a street vendor, where once there was a cheery `thankyou`, there is now at best a grunt.

Or to read the signs of consciousness, not in behaviours but appearances which, perhaps more than anything else, have come to define a sense of `being` in the present time. Concern with appearances, as one strand of materialism, is bound up with an inversion in values relating to the human person. Whereas in the past external physical appearances were viewed as shallow compared with interior qualities, now the external and the visual is the paradigm. The older values, rooted in classical philosophy, having survived more or less for two and a half millennia, have finally been overturned, and replaced by an international and institutionalised fascination with bodies. This concentration on the physical body is expressed most powerfully through various forms of consumption, becoming, as Marx warned, the central component of capitalism and the primary means through which all commodities are absorbed, the body finally itself becoming commoditised as `object`. While this is also self evident in an every day sense, in the display of bodies in their various forms, as clothes hanger, as object for adaptation; to be reshaped, worshipped, decorated, pierced, exchanged, and sold, it is through changing images of bodies in cultural artefacts that we glimpse this relentless exteriorisation. Even the briefest review of how artists have represented bodies over the last hundred years will show both its objectification and fragmentation.

But whatever the symbolic components of a new materialistic consciousness as expressed through the arts, nothing can compare with the brave new scientific reductionism of the new sciences. With their roots in the scientific thinking of the Enlightenment, and driven by neo-Darwinism this combination of `sciences` draws together several strands of ideas including evolutionary psychology, neuro and cognitive sciences, and a genetics based techno-biology. This potently seductive mixture rides high on its technological steed, cracks the genetic code and provides colourful pictures of brains in action. It also fertilises barren women, clones sheep, grows human eggs from aborted foetuses, and defines consciousness in terms of, ` a bundle of neurons`. This blend of ideas is disseminated through high profile media stories, and constitutes a new wave of super- science, marking out the territory for the final phase of human evolution.

The effect of this omni- directional cultural onslaught is to diminish any hold we might have on the belief that there is anything special or unique in being human. The discourses provided by Psychology and Sociology, which have attempted to explain human processes, are surprisingly blunt instruments for the purposes of opening up the human mind. And even in the friendly territory of Psychotherapy, perhaps as one might think, the one remaining place where we might expect to find a residuum for the human person, we find instead complex theorising about selves, and constructs completely bereft of any organic qualities. Whatever the fears for personal survival in an increasingly hostile world, it feels as if all avenues of escape from this cultural wasteland have already been cut off. Slowly but surely progress is demolishing the human soul. Only the lament of a few poets and music makers alert us to the fact that we are the manufacturers of our own extinction. Not only in a physical sense, but also metaphysically and spiritually.

Canto II

THE ROOTS OF discourse about selves and souls reaches back to before Plato, but it is he who has the honour or the blame of dividing humans into two substances, a physical body and non-physical soul, with an explanation, which accounts for the distinction between what is living and what is not. It was this distinction which gave rise to Cartesian dualism twenty centuries later, and which became a Western obsession until the recent present. But between Plato and Descartes the notion of the soul passed through a long series of reconstructions, descriptions and identities. Originally and essentially it was a Greek idea, and essentially foreign to Judaism and Christianity, which only very gradually adopted it. Gradually the two traditions, which fuelled Western culture; the Hebraic and the Hellenic, reformulated the concept of an inner being in their own terms. For example the two Hebrew words, which are used only loosely to depict soul, are *ruach* and *nepesh*. Ruach is rendered as vitality, a description of air in motion, in the form of breath or wind, and nepesh, which literally translates as throat, the channel for breathing, and which is the most reliable sign of life. In this sense, soul is perceived as an invisible dynamic energy, quite simply the breath of life. There was also another word, *leb* that means heart, the beating organ that was the seat of feelings, and which also has resonances with earlier Egyptian beliefs. Together these three terms provided a conceptual basis for

Jewish writers who needed to distinguish between the inner spiritual life and the physical external activities of the body. But the language of the Christian New Testament is Greek, which already carried within itself Platonic philosophical nuances of body and soul. The early Christian writers distinguished between *soma*, which means body, and *sarx* flesh, while spirit as *pneuma* is again seen as a kind of breath, while the soul the inner being is-*psyche*.

By its nature the soul, as an entity or quality, became one of the central concepts of Western philosophy rather than a theological one, although for the ordinary person there would have been no distinction. Whatever their understanding of the soul the laity would have been, informed down the centuries through a semi-literate clergy, in sermons and pictures, and through their own intuitions, for it to eventually become an entirely religious idea. By the time scholastic philosophy was in full swing, the gap between the specialists and the vernacular definitions had become firmly established, and as the Church had a complete monopoly of education, concepts such as the soul and the inner life became synonymous with Christian thinking. But in the history of Western philosophy, there were periods when philosophical speculation moved outside the boundaries set by religious orthodoxy, and it was through these movements that the idea of the `inner life`, the life of the spirit, the soul, assumed a new kind of transcendence, as the means of escaping the fetters of institutional control. It was not so much through the church then, but through oppositional philosophy that these pockets of resistance came to stimulate western art and western sensibilities. And it was through this broader cultural exposure, through the works of musicians, poets and painters, that art and the aesthetic experience became the interpreters of the soul for the ordinary person, identifying it as the source of creativity and the means of transcendence. One result of this in the present, at an everyday level of thinking, is that notions of soul have become vague, and beyond definition. And have become confused in popular imagination with several other concepts, which describe a deeply embedded sense of self. In fact the terms, self, identity, and personality are used interchangeably, often with the assumption that they refer to the same thing.

This confusion is itself part of a complex history of competing ideas, in which the fight for the frontiers of knowledge have been fought over by armies of philosophers, scientists, ideologues, and artists. In philosophy, since Descartes redefined the dual nature of being, there has been a continuous attack on the soul, as if this were the defining feature separating the old from the new, the past from the future. This began with the Renaissance, and progressed through the Reformation, the Enlightenment, and Nineteenth Century Scientism, through Modernism to so-called Post-Modernism.

At the start of this period, the idea of the human person was elevated to the status of being the measure of all things, celebrated by Da Vinci, Michael Angelo, Raphael, Erasmus, More, Bacon, and others. Through architecture, art and music they crystallised their visions of the protean self. But these signals of transcendence reached their zenith with the new cosmology, and the scientific revolution of Copernicus and Galileo, which removed the tiny planet Earth from the centre of the universe, and by implication the centrality of humankind from the central axis of creation. From there on the trajectory of the status of the human person was downward, culminating in the nineteenth century of Comte, Mill, Darwin, Nietzsche, Marx, and Freud. This final phase described by Comte as the progress of human history from a mythical and theological condition, through a metaphysical and abstract period, to a triumphant positivistic and scientific arrival of true humanity. But through this evolutionary and social process of becoming modern, humans had lost their souls, both actually and metaphorically, and apart from a Romantic resistance to this, all that was required to complete this process was the means of redefining what it was to be human.

The new thinking came with Darwin, Marx and Freud, each contributing to an exciting new paradigm of humanity, as an evolved rational economic species. Freed from superstition and enchantment, but dwarfed by an ever burgeoning massing of society, to become alienated and anonymous depersonalised abstractions .By the time that the main tenets of Freud's psychodynamic theory of personality had been absorbed, modern society had already succumbed to the combined power of science, in the form of technology, and capitalism as the twin poles of human progress, fuelling wars and consumerism.

But progress in the form of scientific materialism was unable to completely eliminate a metaphysical element in modern thought. A powerful reaction in the form of artistic resistance emerged, and writers, dramatists, painters and poets became the dedicated guardians of the soul, against scientific and materialistic reductionism. Freud became aware of this resistance, and built it into his theories, while at the same time claiming scientific status for his own ideas. Freud's ambiguity in this has led to suggestions that he was attempting to redefine the nature of souls. Bettelheim (1982) argues that in English translations of Freud`s works, the German word *seele* is rendered as `mind`, and not as soul, and that this basic mistake has changed the whole emphasis of Freud`s intentions. Bettelheim explains further that Freud refers to psychoanalysis as the `science of the soul`, as meaning a way of tending the most valuable part of a person, and that Freud `s preference for this term rested on its range of meaning, its emotional resonances, its intangible qualities, and its roots in the mind's earliest primordial mythic essences.

If Freud's intentions were in fact frustrated by inadequate translation, then this has the most serious implications for the whole development and history of Western psychology. But even more so for psychotherapy, for all modern psychotherapeutic approaches are in some way direct reflections of Freud's Psychodynamic theories, or responses to and rejections of them. The puzzle, as Bettelheim remarks, is that despite the many complex allusions to `soul` throughout his writing, Freud does not provide a precise working definition, but is vague and ambiguous. The reason possibly is because ultimately it is beyond definition, and perhaps also it is because of this ambiguity, which best captures the souls sublime fragile insubstantiality, that he preferred it. But if we are to attempt to search further, perhaps to glimpse the images Freud was reaching for, we have to imagine some of the many examples referred to in his letters, and his style of reflective thinking. A kind of Socratic dialogue with himself while experiencing ordinary everyday occurrences. Perhaps while observing the effects of light filtered through trees, or casting shadows through the windows of his study. Whatever the shades of meaning, the resonances are ancient Greek, subterranean, and not religious, for Freud the soul is deeply embedded, active, organic, autonomous, reflexive, and sublime How else could he express it? And if souls themselves are not immortal, then the concept itself is, for despite its adversaries since Socrates, it alone drives the imagination and delivers us from being mere matter.

Canto III

CASUAL READERS OF Plato (if there are such) might
assume that the concentration on souls throughout his
works show that his ideas were common knowledge to the
ordinary Athenian, and that people thought of themselves
in terms of souls, but this was not the case. Cornford, in
his published lectures, points out that `ordinary Atheni-
ans` tended to be rather vague about souls or inner selves,
and usually referred to themselves in terms of their bodies,
and that it was for this reason that philosophers needed to
discover the soul`s secrets and how to care for the soul. In
the *Phaedo* Socrates identifies the `true self` as the soul,
and that the source of happiness is in perfecting the soul,
in other words making one's soul as good as possible. Certainly, through quietening one's mind and avoiding worry,
but also by being reflective and conscious of relationships,
and having a `cool` sense of being.

But curiosity about the soul was not some pointless
arcane philosophical exercise; it was understood as part of
a wider debate about the means to happiness, good health,
and well-being. During the first century AD, the blending
of cultures as a consequence of Roman occupation of the
Middle East produced a wide array of `experimental`
communities. One of these groups, identified by Philo
Judaeus from Alexandria, as *therapeutae* and *therapeutrides*

applied psychotherapeutic methods to body and soul, in the cure of,"…terrible and almost incurable diseases, which pleasures and appetites, fears and griefs, and covetousness, and follies, and injustice, and all the rest of innumerable multitude of other passions and vices, have inflicted upon them." This was not some obscure cult, but a widely distributed movement, which followed a particular life-style connected with healing, and sharing their knowledge of techniques and methods of healing. Foucault also mentions *therapeutae* in an essay (1988), emphasising the relationship between the Delphic principle " Know Thy Self" and an imperative for taking care of yourself, pointing out that,

"When you take care of the body, you don't take care of the self. The self is not clothing, tools, or possessions. It is to be found in the principle, which uses these tools, a principle not of the body but of the soul. You have to worry about your soul - that is the principle activity of caring for yourself."

It is worth noting that these earliest psychotherapeutic practioners made a distinction between selves, souls, and bodies, and that selves were surface attributes, in modern terms the outcome of socialisation, manifesting themselves through physical actions and agency. But souls were something deeper, perceived as a person's essence, their life force, and the real source of their vitality. For Plato all three were combined as parts or `faculties` of what we would understand as personality, in his terms: the body, reasoning, and spirit, and these being driven by three basic drives; a person's physiological appetites, feelings, and thoughts. This might have provided a template for Freud, for there are ancient echoes in Freud's psychodynamic theory of personality, and an uncanny resemblance to Plato's tripartite psyche. For Freud's model of personality also has three dimensions, the basic earthly ID, with its urges and desires, the EGO, the reality principle, reasoning with the unreasonable instinctive demands of the id, while the SUPER-EGO, the conscience, guardian of our moral being. For Freud there are also the ancient resonances that the source of illness is a malaise of the soul, and not purely physical but always psychosomatic, a consequence of bad `humours`, ruptured relationships, grief and sadness. But his quest for scientific respectability required that these nuances were translated into `modern` terms, as evidenced in his essay, `Project for a Scientific Psychology` sent to Fliess in 1895. It was also his impulse for scientific respectability that created the rift between Jung and himself, because the `basic differences in assumptions` that Jung admits, concerned Jung's fascination with the soul.

The reaction to Psychoanalysis came in the form of hard-edged positivism, with the theories of Pavlov, Watson, and later B.F.Skinner. Behaviourism was made for the *Brave New World*, and was championed by philosophers such as Gilbert Ryle and A J Ayer, and the group known as the `Vienna Circle`; (Carnap,Feigl, Schlick, and others) It was during the period between 1909 and the 1960s, that the language of the *Self* displaced that of the *Soul*. Although theories of the Self had been around for a long time, for example the Scottish Philosopher Hume had seen it as a bundle of different perceptions (viewpoints), it was Behaviouristic Psychology, and modern Sociology that elevated it as the standard Western model of the Human Person.

One of the earliest Psychologists to put forward views about the self was William James, who described it as a product of all the different relationships a person has with other people,: " A man has as many selves as there are individuals who recognise him and carry an image of him in their minds." In this sense, the Self is not owned by the individual person, but constitutes an interface between the discrete individual and society. It has no psychological depth but is a social product, its essence no deeper than a list of descriptions. James also was the first to distinguish between the `I` of subjective experience, and the `me` as an object of knowledge, a distinction which was to influence later theories of self, and which has become the foundation of all modern psychotherapies. There is an interesting cultural twist to this paradigmatic shift, this flip over from soul to selves, most clearly observed in the writings of James, for James had a deep philosophical interest in the inner life, and was sympathetic to traditional notions of spirituality. Prior to James`s theorising about selves, almost every Western Philosopher contributed to discussions about the soul. Following James`s distinction between I and Me, the philosophical territory dedicated to `being` and `persons`, was claimed by the social sciences, Sociology, Psychology, and Anthropology, and with that accession passed over new obligations, for every social theorist to contribute to and defend the new model of being, the Self.

Charles Horton, Cooley, James and George Herbert Mead, were the founders of a new way of looking at persons, providing the intellectual foundations for theorising about that inner core that we once quaintly called the soul. Cooleys `Looking Glass Self` became the model for Goffmans more recent studies of the self, which in turn became the stimulus for novels, such as `One Flew over the cuckoos nest. Berger and Luckmanns sociological studies highlighted the social construction of reality, of which the `self` is just one aspect, while anthropologists demonstrated the cultural relativism of the concept. But the greatest growth in theorising about self was from the burgeoning social work and psychotherapy industry.

Canto IV

THE WIDE VARIETY of activities, ideas and beliefs that constitute psychotherapy is so vast that it is difficult to comprehend how all of these can be accommodated within a single framework with one single defining label. But psychotherapy in this sense is a broad generic category which has evolved and adjusted to various social and cultural influences, and continues to adapt and adjust to new influences from almost every other human activity.

Among the more recent influences is what might best be described as a `faith-based spirituality`. But spirituality is not like other influences which have produced distinctive types of therapy, such as music and art and drama, although each of these might be regarded as spiritual in some sense. Spirituality per se is in a category all of its own where psychotherapy is concerned.

One of the reasons psychotherapy is hesitant to whole heartedly embrace spirituality is that throughout its long journey towards recognition as a serious way of `healing` people, it has had to chart a careful route between science and `religiosity`, for want of a better term. Perhaps the term religiosity is not entirely suitable here, but it seems to sum up the strange combination of serious-minded spiritual seeking and a simple-minded other worldliness that has hung around on the periphery of psychotherapy from time to time throughout its development.

It is worth recalling that Freud`s psychodynamic theories which became the prototype for the whole of psychotherapy were nurtured partly as a reaction to Kraepelin`s inflexible psychiatric model, and also against some of the most bizarre expressions of European spirituality such as Madame Blavatsky`s Theosphical Society (1884), the Society for Psychical Research, the Synthetic Society, and the even more famous Metaphysical Society, to mention only a few, which by then had become part of the resistance against an equally bizarre materialism and scientism. It was against this cultural and intellectual background that the disputes between the early founders of modern psychotherapy were fought, between Freud, Adler and Jung, as they attempted to define the boundaries of their own differing approaches. Consequently the guardians of psychotherapy have held an ambivalent defence against the intrusion of a full-blown transcendent spirituality.

This ambivalence is best characterised as a door neither open nor closed, but ajar, neither embracing nor denying spirituality as part of the psychotherapeutic framework, but leaving the whole discourse, debate, or questions suspended. To some extent this has merely reflected wider social developments, but it also reveals a deep neuroses concerning spirituality within the central ideas and beliefs in psychotherapy. And this neurosis is the outcome of a double ambivalence, towards science and religion, the twin poles between which European thinking has reverberated since the Enlightenment in the 17th century.

Until fairly recently, the guiding influences in psychotherapy have been able to maintain an aloof mid-position between these two poles, but as Faith-based demands, from both new practioners and clients have increased this has produced palpitations in some members of the psychotherapeutic family. Their fears are not so much that there will be a dilution of established practice and standards, as one might imagine, but that spirituality simply is at odds with what they understand psychotherapy to be. And that if at some time it got its foot in the door, it would shift everything, seriously challenging some of the long cherished values and tenets at the core of psychotherapy. But most importantly and significantly it would call into question ideas and beliefs of what constitutes the human person, for these are the basis on which all other assumptions about psychotherapy are assembled.

Present day psychotherapy has come a long way since Freud. The psychoanalytic model of personality has been dismantled and reassembled many times and in many different ways, so much so that our current models of self are complex constructions, made to reflect a need to work within mainstream health care paradigms. But faith-based approaches operate within completely different paradigms, the essential difference depending on dualism, which states that persons are a combination of body and soul. Psychotherapy has few problems with bodies, but it cannot deal with souls. In fact Freud and the other founding fathers of psychotherapy established their business on the premise that souls did not exist, or that if they do, they are outside the business of psychotherapy.

Ken Evans

This is a problem for psychotherapists, who have personal beliefs about souls, and perhaps in many cases for practicing psychotherapists, some will separate their professional and their personal beliefs, and understandably these personal beliefs will influence their ways of working. And in cases where both therapist and client share a common belief, then surely this is no problem. But if at some point souls were allowed in at a more general level, then both theory and practice would change very considerably.

I can visualise the effects of this discussion on some practicing psychotherapists that I know. Some will be amused, some dismissive, and others confused, perhaps most will be confused because the way they use language permits them to hold very loose and vague definitions of `self`, which "kind of flows" into other notions of personhood, and which perhaps sometimes touches on something very much like souls. So what is the problem they will ask? Well the problem is that Selves and Souls are not the same things, although in some psychotherapy literature there is the same kind of ambiguity mentioned above.

Selves are socially constructed models or frameworks which reflect the social economic and political needs of society rather than describing the central core of being. Selves are what social identity is all about. Souls, on the other hand, constitute the non-physical attributes of a person's uniqueness, and as a concept is not necessarily linked to any particular belief system, religious paradigm or doctrine. In fact it is more a philosophical concept than a religious one.

For the whole of the psychotherapy enterprise to readjust to the idea of souls it would require a more philosophical and anthropological approach during psychotherapy training. It would also mean that students would need to engage more with the ideas of what distinguishes humans from other animals, and with ideas and theories of consciousness, and to develop new approaches of engaging the inner person.

This would mean that psychotherapy training would need to become more academically rigorous and more critical, and more reflexive than it is at present. But it would still need to resist the dogmatism and the intransigence of fundamentalistic beliefs, and still pursue a middle course, the via media, but receptive to people who need both psychotherapy and care for their souls.

Canto V

Modern Western societies have adjusted to the demographic changes during the last fifty years or so, by replacing informal institutional processes with formal agencies, social care is now as widely available as medical care. Many of the small daily intimacies, which confirmed a sense of being at a personal level, within families and neighbourhoods, are either not available, or have been replaced by substitutes provided by `Caring ` agencies. The provision of social care in its various forms, besides responding to the changing shape of society, has also played an active part in those changes through its various political agendas, currently the so-called `Modernisation` strategy. The various agencies, mainly the Social Services, employ processes and procedures intended to assist individuals and families when they are unable to cope themselves, and frequently take over where medical provision stops, for example when someone is discharged from hospital. But they also attempt to deal with more subtle emotional problems relating to the quality of inner life, in personal relationships, family breakdown, various forms of abuse, elderly care, and so on. The skills they apply are structured from sociological and psychological abstracts, but fashioned according to one of several models of social work practice, nearly all of which assume that there is a problem to be solved. The operating framework of local authority statutory services, (those services that must be provided by law) is bureaucratic, and has a tendency to draw on examples of practice from medical agencies, sometimes the language of the practioners is identical. There is also a pyramid of informal (care) agencies, which attempt to fill in the gaps of formal provision; mainly residential care, in their attempt to be `professional` they too borrow the terminology of the `statutory` system. From whatever agency, their procedures in dealing with the public, are formalised and as far as possible, `safe`, first and foremost legally safe, clinically safe, etc. , this and the other shared rules under which they operate, tends to identify them as all part of a system. A system potentially with its fingers touching people at the most tender and painful and vulnerable points in their lives, using techniques and methodologies fashioned by the briefest acquaintance of `selves`. For usually social intervention is intensely practical, spoken for according to budgets. The complexity of how persons see themselves, and which might be the fundamental cause of their `problem`, is beyond the system. There can be no work with selves, for this is psycho-social therapy territory. And here is yet another structure, another system, more refined and further removed from everyday life. For to gain access its services via psychological assessment contributes to its perceived elevated status, for while it does not deal with the soul, it is seen as touching the mind. And the mind in everyday terms is something more complicated than the body, still mysterious, beyond comprehension and discussion of ordinary people.

What then of the self ? If indeed Psychotherapy is the last bastion in defence of the `Self `, the guardians of the sanctity of the concept of the `Human Person`, how safe is it in their hands? If the answer depends on how their aspirations coincide with those of the *Therapeutae* of the first century, and even this was positive, then the answer would still be mixed. For twenty first century psychotherapy is not fashioned on the Socratic admonition that one should, first and foremost, care for the soul. And even if there is, at times, an agnostic inclination to at least include thoughts of souls in their thinking, even the most spiritual therapists will avoid openly declaring that this might be what they are doing. For Psychotherapy is a broad `Church`, with its feet in the various modern personality theories of Freud, Behaviourism, and Humanism, with many of its mainstream variations utilising analytical ideas, and with many offshoots and branches, mixing and matching. Sometimes eclectically combining strands of Western and non-Western thinking, sometimes defiantly mechanistic in its application of Behaviour Modification, while at the other end of the scale, applying séance –like therapeutic processes of regression to moments at birth and even before. In some approaches the `self ` will be central, in others it will be an unstated element in the `process`. But the field is not short of discussion about `self`, and the range of literature, ranging from philosophic controversies, through cognitive and neuroscientific models, developmental, humanistic, analytical, phenomenological; to meditational, and metaphysical, continues to explore the ultimately indefinable.

The simple answer to the question posed, is that as long as discussion about `self` continues, there is still the flickering flame of `soul`, which underpins for the ordinary person, a sense of being. For some psychotherapies which fasten on the centrality of the self, as the focus of their intervention, the *self* becomes soul-like, the essential character of personhood, not a social construction, but a real existential thing, embodied but not physical, but not mystical either. The difficulty of any discourse about selves is in the different approaches; those that include philosophical sympathies will most likely construct evolutionary models, in which selves include cultural remnants of soul-like characteristics. While for those whose affiliation is to the scientific, their models of self will be built around neuropsychology and cognitive sciences. But how these models are applied is another matter, and it is this that is the crucial problem in the application of psychotherapy, for the informed assumptions of the practioners are unlikely to coincide with the beliefs and understanding of therapees, and this disjunction in understanding and attitudes most likely accounts for any ineffectiveness of psychotherapeutic intervention. For the gap between professional theorising, and its practical application, strikes at the centre of the process, the interaction of two individuals, in the giving and receiving of love, (for want of a better word), and that gap being defined in terms of empathy, quite literally an `empathy gap`. And while we have increasingly come to accept this empathy gap in our daily interactions, and perhaps view it as a change in public manners, and even accept it in routine health and social care visits, we baulk at the idea that it should occur at the outer limits of human experience, when dealing with matters of life and death, of mental exhaustion, of emotional pain, of madness and despair. This theme of 'empathy gaps' represents the lynchpin, the hinge of the flow of ideas between science and other discourses, between science and capitalism, science and art, science and nature, etc, and is characterised in various forms of resistance to so-called scientific advancement.

At the point that modern science and technology started to bite, at the earliest stages of industrialisation, there was an intuitive resistance by ordinary people, who could sense the dark shadows of the machine, as representative of industrial capitalism, to the possibilities of enslavement and to its dominance, to the squeezing out of their humanity. To them their only means of survival, despite their frenzied attacks, was by befriending the machine, and eventually themselves becoming machine -like. This resistance, often ridiculed by historians as simple-minded Ludditeism, gave way to Romanticism, which became the dominant form of artistic protest against the diminution of the soul. But Romanticism was seen by some as egotistical, as focusing too much on individualism, and became enmeshed in the 'politics of sharing', of socialism and communism, which in turn produced its own psychological reactions, commonly termed Personalism.

Nicholas Berdyaev was one of Personalism's leading exponents, banished from Soviet Russia because of his opposition to State Communism, he developed an existential philosophy which focused on persons as primarily and essentially creative beings, which sets humans apart from other species. But his philosophy views 'human creativity' only as a potential, for it is through it that we overcome our natural disposition to slavery. In his terms, slavery takes many forms, for example the pursuit of power or wealth for their own sake is to become enslaved, or mindlessly following a religion, or worse still to become totally socialised into society, is to become enslaved by civilisation and technique, a predisposition towards totalitarian control. His main resistance to science was based on the view that science had contributed to human control, it was deterministic, and it was based on one kind of thinking, rejecting emotions and other sensitivities such as intuition. Other Personalists, such as Emmanuel Mournier developed a following of these ideas across Europe through a monthly journal, *Esprit* (1932), and the publication of a *Personalists Manifesto*, and through it encouraged a resistance to Capitalism, Fascism, Communism, and all other forms of state control, arguing for local communities and decentralisation. During the Second World War, Esprit was sufficiently influential to merit suppression by Petain, with Mounier and others imprisoned, which in turn led to Esprit groups joining the resistance, demonstrating that the movement was more than some mere esoteric clique.

In America Lewis Mumford was arguing along similar lines, he identified the depersonalisation of the individual as the most threatening aspect of American capitalism, as a process that would one day reap its own harvest. Other writers at this time, such as Aldous Huxley, Max Scheler, Jaques Maritain, Martin Buber, and Karl Mannheim, who were aware of increasing state control, identified the consequences in one way or another as the diminishing of the human spirit. Erich Fromm, in `The Fear of Freedom `(1942) provides a vivid image of how deeply this was felt at the every day level.

"The extent to which the average person in America is filled with the same sense of fear and insignificance seems to find a telling expression in the fact of the popularity of the Mickey Mouse pictures. There the one theme-in so many variations-is always this: something little is persecuted and endangered by something overwhelmingly strong, which threatens to kill or swallow the little thing. The little thing runs away and eventually succeeds in escaping or even in harming the enemy. People would not be ready to look continually at the many variations of this one theme unless it touched upon something very close to their own emotional life."

Canto VI

IT MAY WELL be that the Soul is a figment of the imagination, that it exists only as an idea. Whether or not that is the case, we have no way of knowing, and anyway the distinction does not matter, for the consequences to us are exactly the same. Whether it is real or imagined, the soul has occupied a central place in our thinking for more than four millennia, and it continues to exert a powerful, but hidden influence in the way ordinary people think about themselves. During that enormous period of time it has been the primary focus of complete civilisations and for others the central tenet of its cultural philosophy. For Europeans, it has been the dominant source of inspiration for the whole of Western culture and philosophy; it has placed humans above all other forms of life, and provided the sole channel through which our sense of the numinous has been communicated. If it is only an idea then it has sustained life on a level beyond the merely mundane and physical, and enabled us to transcend the limits of our mortality.

It has also been ridiculed and trashed, attached to movements and beliefs that have died or are dying, been rejected, hacked about, translated and relentlessly redefined, and in the current climate, relinquished to the dustbin of obsolete ideas. Almost but not quite, for despite its main scientific objection being its immateriality, ironically the same objection applies to the concepts of `self`, and `consciousness`, and if these are admitted then so also is `soul`. One imagines, with the same sense of triumph of those who cheered Mickey Mouse, the frustrations of the hard-bitten scientists, who in their inability to claim their complete and final victory over the eradication of the soul, like Rumplestiltskin tearing themselves apart.

And where Philosophy, and Theology, and Sociology, and Psychology, and Psycho-social therapeutic theorising has failed to make sense of soul, the Arts and artists have held firm, resisting the political and economic forces that regard the soul as, merely nothing, or frighteningly, as the premier symbol of resistance. And that resistance is expressed through the language of aesthetics, through the visible and invisible arts, through painting, sculpture, music, dance, poetry, and literature, for the creative source of these is held to be beyond both heart and mind; they are the language of the soul. For what other possible reason would we raise the arts above all other human achievements and aspirations? They touch us beyond the senses, move us and sustain us, offer meaning in a meaningless world, and energise us in the depth of our Being, what other language can we possibly use to describe this experience; or do we say that something has moved our `self`, our `personality`, our `social identity`? To the artist the soul is sublime and euphoric; it sings.

The creative impulse is experienced as something distinctively internal, something felt to be separate from a person's biology, a level of being that needs to realise itself, with its compulsion to create for no other purpose than to express itself. When we attempt to understand this, we search for rational explanations, because that is what analytical thinking demands, but if all art emanates from the soul, then the explanation is in the art itself, and ultimately beyond critical explanation. This has been the central message of philosophers who have attempted to explain art, and it is how artists themselves understand it. When the Symbolist painter Gustave Moreau claimed that he had faith, ` only in what I do not see, and solely in what I feel.`, he was aligning himself with sympathies of other Romantic artists and writers, who sought a reality only visible to the inner eye, the eye of the soul. For Edgar Allan Poe, this was explicitly expressed in his, ` The Poetic Principle`, a theory of poetry he based on an idea that the human self is composed of, intellect, conscience, and soul. For him the intellect is concerned with truth, conscience with duty, and the soul with beauty. And since poetry, and by association all other art is produced by the soul, art has no responsibility other than to reach out to other souls, to excite and comfort them, sharing beauty according to their needs.

The Symbolist painters; Odilon Redon and Gustave Moreau, along with the Pre-Raphaelites; Burn-Jones, Rossetti, the Nabi painters, Paul Serusier, Maurice Denis and Edouard Vuillard, and the Romantic poets; Blake, Colerdge, Wordsworth, Shelley and Keats, worked and spoke with a desperate intensity, knowing that all of the social, political, and economic forces of their civilisation were cooperating to eliminate the soul. Their desperation in that knowledge, that they perhaps were fighting a rearguard and final action, against enormous odds, for the survival of mans soul, concentrated their minds, producing an incandescent art that threatened to burn the senses. It is possible to sense both the fear and anguish with Wordsworth in his "Intimations of Immortality from Recollection of Early Childhood", and the impending sense of loss of; "the glory and freshness of a dream", the, "visionary gleam", "the celestial light", in two brief stanzas from the Ode.

"Turn whersoe`er I may,
By Night or day,
The things which I have seen I now can see no more;"
And
"But yet I know, where`er I go,
That there hath past away a glory from the earth."

The relationship between artists and ordinary persons has its own history, with the artist sometimes viewed as genius, or mad, or just different. Whatever the real differences, it is their excessive creativity which permits them to speak on our behalf, to let their souls speak for ours, and to share in the triumph of their creativity; because to hear, and see, and touch their creations, is to experience something that resonates with our own creativity. For whatever else art is, it is a channel of communication not of the senses, or minds, or selves, but between souls. Art is also the most profound means of healing, as E.M. Forster has insisted. " The Arts are not drugs. They are not guaranteed to act when taken. Something as mysterious and capricious as the creative impulse has to be released before they can act."

But when we become sick we reach for the products of science, in the form of chemicals and drugs, because we bodily locate the cause of our illness and identify a specific medicine that treats the symptoms. For most of us, we do not know how the medicines work, as long as it makes us better. But as Oliver Sacks argues, making people better has a `metaphysical` dimension, and that curing is concerned with dealing with, " One's ontological organisation, one's entire being - for all its multiplicity, all its shimmering, ever- shifting succession of patterns." In reference to the patients he was treating (those with *encephalitis lethargica*-sleeping sickness) to go beyond mere chemicals, and even beyond , " `Deep` accommodation, rest, care, ingenuity,…" Beyond the organisation of care, to something, "… more important than all of them, and perhaps a prerequisite for all of them, is the establishment of a proper relation with the world, and in particular- with other human beings." And that is through relationships with others that," One sees that the beautiful and ultimate metaphysical truth, which has been stated by poets and physicians and metaphysicians in all ages-by Leibniz and Donne and Dante and Freud: that Eros is the oldest and strongest of the gods; that love is the *alpha* and *omega* of being; and that the work of healing, of rendering whole, is, first and last, the business of love." It surely needs no explanation that love with all its mysterious power cannot work directly on bodies, but via the ancient route through the contact between souls.

Canto VII

THE SURVIVAL OF the concept of Soul has implications that go beyond our sense of Being, our good health, beyond art, and even beyond life itself. For in what other terms can we account for the sentiments which surround those who have died, and their remains, which we still sometimes refer to as mortal, concealing the notion that there might also be, at the very least a hint of a hint, an immortal component. While it might be reasonably simple to account for the spontaneous amassing of flowers at roadside shrines, marking the spot of someone's death, it is less obvious, in our materialistic age, that so much outrage should be directed at hospitals for storing body parts, or the stacking of corpses on unrefridgerated floors, when space in the hospital mortuary runs out. Unless of course, there is a residual belief, that humans, even dead humans are more than just lumps of meat. During the last few years, from time to time, the national media has run stories about parents who have grieved for a dead child, only to discover that one or more of their dead child's organs has been stored by a hospital in which the child died. And that this discovery required further grieving, and the various body parts brought together. There have also been reports of cases where people have died in extreme situations, on mountain tops, or in submarines at impossible depths, requiring huge effort and costs to recover their remains. It is easy to explain at one level that this is necessary for closure, but the passions that are aroused by these stories suggest something deeper, that death is a focal point which activates the deepest recesses of our unconscious, reverberating all that we know about life and death, and about loss and separation. These stories, usually accompanied by disturbing photographs of anonymous corpses, act as modern `memento mori` -- literally reminders of our own inevitable end.

What they also show is our ambivalence towards bodies, our own and other's. On the one hand the notion that the body is all, while on the other, that what it leaves behind after death, is more than our memories of the deceased; more than the physical signs and marks left by the body's one time presence, and physical evidence of its agency. Somehow much more than this, but less physical.

There is an interesting idea in Walter Benjamin`s `Art in the age of mechanical reproduction`, which distinguishes the original work of art from it's many reproductions, which he calls it's *aura*. He clarifies this in terms of, " The authenticity of a thing that is the essence of all that is transmissible from its beginning, ranging from its substantive duration to its testimony to the history which it has experienced." If we can think in terms of objects having an aura, then more so the authentic person. In which case, what remains after death is a deceased person's aura, their vacant space, their creations, their odours, their presence, in short, their stamp on the world, undeniably more than the physical evidence of being here, and much more than memories, to some peoples minds, something very much like a soul.

Canto VIII

THE STATUS OF the idea of the soul in modern times is tenuous, for the majority of the population the belief that each one of them possesses an invisible and immortal soul is not only meaningless, but has no relevance to how they live their daily lives. For the majority, they will only encounter the word in films and songs and even then it will not make any demands on their thoughts or imagination. For them the word stands as a cipher equivalent to ghost or spirit and for the few, it might just have some vague nostalgic value.

At school they will encounter it in poetry and in their brief brush with Shakespeare, and again it will be incomprehensible, but they will be equally mystified by modern counterfeit theories of self and personality. Ironically for this generation that wishes most to be understood, they lack even the most basic conceptual framework for self- reflection.

But there was a time in Western civilisation when the Soul occupied the centre of ordinary peoples thinking, not in any complex intellectual way, but as common knowledge. Up until the Reformation, not only had the Soul as an idea gathered an increasing amount of cultural baggage, but it had also become a commodity, to be bought and sold, and as such it was this which was the start of its diminution.

In the middle ages the Catholic Church had acquired vast wealth across the whole of Europe, and had come to resemble a multi-national corporation with thousands of franchised outlets. What was on sale at each of these outlets, in the form of indulgencies, was forgiveness and redemption, not only for the souls of the living but also for souls of the dead and departed. None of this would have been possible without the whole population's devotion to the Soul. It is common-place to view this historical period principally in terms of high politics and corruption within the Church and to ignore the social and cultural significance of what the Church provided at individual and personal levels.

The Church through each of its local outlets provided the means of sustaining vitality of each individual's souls. In fact the franchise was basically for the care of souls through the Eucharist at the weekly mass, which in pre-Reformation England had become a therapeutic event. In contrast to the monotony of daily grinding work, the mass provided; comforting words, spectacle, drama, atmosphere and resolution to fears, worries and concerns. The walls of even the smallest parish churches were painted in brilliant colours, there was music and poetry which reverberated with a deep and profound reality, there was incense and candles, and homilies and sermons to stimulate their thoughts, and mystery plays. The total effect was exhilarating, uplifting, and sustaining.

But the Reformation brought the sudden demolition of all this for doctrinal reasons beyond the understanding of ordinary people, to be enforced by the severest sanctions.

Shrines and Holy places were destroyed, and relics and sacred images were defiled, the familiar liturgy which brought comfort and solace to the bereaved was revised, constituted a form of cultural cleansing. This doctrinal and physical destruction left a massive social and emotional vacuum which struck at the heart and soul of every local community. In the North of England 40, 000 Pilgrims of Grace challenged the King's claim to Royal (spiritual) Supremacy.

The impact on the common people of this wanton destruction of traditional spiritual habits must have been more traumatic than is generally understood, causing a demand for alternative means of nurturing the soul. For the educated elite there was the new `Metaphysical Poetry of Donne and others, but for the common people the main source of this was theatre and the new plays of Shakespeare and Marlow; both of these writers knowing the public mood and responding to their need for an alternative route for spiritual expression. While Marlow made the purchasing of souls in Faustus a terrible thing, Shakespeare helped to maintain the belief in the continuity of the soul between this world and the next. In Hamlet, Macbeth and Richard the Third nothing would make sense without the intervention of ghosts, and their part in the stories reinforced the audience's common understanding of their presence and influence. But in `Hamlet` Shakespeare goes further and reminds his audience of some basic theological truths of the old order. Although the outlawed term "Purgatory" is never directly mentioned Hamlet's father's Ghost clearly implies that he has returned from Purgatory, and is, "Doomed for a certain term to walk the night / And for the day confined to fast in fires, / Till the foul crimes done in days of nature / Are burnt and purged away" (1.5.11-14). Even the idea of transubstantiation is aired in a disguised conundrum ,when Hamlet tells Claudius; "A man may fish with a worm that hath eat of a king, and eat of the fish that had fed of that worm," thus "a king may go a progress through the guts of a beggar" (4.3.27-32). This was a cryptic reference to the real fear of a consecrated host (the small round wafer of unleavened bread) being eaten by an animal, which in effect would be tantamount to the actual body of Jesus being eaten by a non-Christian. Besides this the plays are scattered with oaths sworn on the names of Saints, and there are many tiny theological references which served to remind and comfort an audience starved of the communion with the souls of their departed loved ones.

These coded messages now fall on the deaf ears of a generation a million miles from their home!

Canto VIIII

PART OF THE attractiveness of psychology as an academic subject is that it holds out the promise of revealing something hidden about ourselves. Just as before the emergence of modern psychology, this same impulse, this desire for self-knowledge, had been expressed through myth, religious text, and philosophy. According to Kuhn`s theory of `Scientific Revolutions`, which attempts to explain how new ideas supplant old, modern psychologists should be thinking in a completely different way to the past, not just in terms of different language and concepts, but with a completely different paradigm. In some aspects of psychology they have succeeded, but in attempting to explain who we are, questions directed at Identity, Self, Personality, and Consciousness, modern psychology has failed to make much progress. At a fundamental level of theorising, evident in basic levels of description, the problems are the same, and the quest for answers to questions about ourselves are just as elusive as ever.

For example the ancient search for the location of the soul has now become the search for the self, which for some theorists is equally ethereal, being merely a `social construct`, and therefore equally mysterious. But besides the apparent shift in language, which masks the similarities between selves and souls rather than reveal the differences, there are other interesting ploys that unintentionally or unconsciously link past and present thinking. One very trivial example illustrates this; the use of pictures of the human brain to illustrate discussions about minds. These pictures look the same in books old and new, as might be expected but what is particularly interesting about their use as illustrations is their purpose. Rather than contribute to discussions about who and what we are, these strange illustrations of brains, offer no clues what so ever about how anything works. Quite the reverse in fact, for they only add to the mystery, by suggesting that somehow perhaps the real me, my inner core might reside in one form or another, within the convoluted coils of grey matter.

But what really links the past with the present, and perhaps lies behind the use of brain illustrations is the belief that our sense of self, formerly our soul, actually has a physical location, which in European cultures has always been somewhere within the brain. The earliest pre-Socratic speculations were that the soul resides in one of the inner spaces, the cavities or ventricles, as they became known. Plato, Strato, Hippocrates, and Hippolytus each identified one of these spaces as the home of the soul. Much later Descartes located it in the pineal gland, while Galen identified the fourth ventricle, Mundinus, a famous anatomist of the middle ages, claimed that it was the third ventricle, while St. Augustine thought that it was the middle ventricle. The choice of ventricles, or cavities was chosen because they resembled rooms, places with space for the pneuma, the gaseous substance, to move and expand.

This strange primitive fascination with location continues currently in the form of brain scanning techniques, which attempt to interpret brain activity, essentially attempts to capture thoughts through signs of increased blood flow, and so continues a primitive tradition of believing and searching for the invisible in the visible, the metaphysical in the physical. But to identify this belief as primitive is not to deride it as simplistic, quite the reverse, for the complexity of mind and thought has not yet revealed to modern science how we, as persons inhabit the `spaces` of our imaginations, or how or why this became possible with the emergence of consciousness. All we have is the conundrum of having a sense of being which intuitively we locate somewhere within, and the thoughts and ideas of curious minds from the past which have attempted to prod for answerers. And when we read them closely, we attempt the impossible in trying to re-enter the spaces of their thoughts. All we know is that they inhabited a more permissive world of thought, where real physical spaces coallesequed with metaphorical, allegorical, and metaphysical space, permitting them comfortably to occupy two spheres of existence, and the freedom to move from one to the other without contradiction.

The ventricles, the seat of the soul, were both physical and metaphysical, and consequently real physical spaces were modelled accordingly. Arguably the most basic feature of any culture is its purposive use of space, how it is captured, enclosed and used, and by extension how it shapes the rest of culture, in the spaces between the sounds that make its language, the spaces between individual persons, their activities, events, and between the actual and the imagined, and so on. From the earliest times this sense of space was expressed in terms of proximity and distance, as evidenced in the Neolithic cave `hands paintings`, and in the great temple cultures of India and the Middle East, and later in Greece and Rome. To understand this, as a process requires a reversed style of thinking as applied in the case of tracing the roots of Western architecture by the various Renaissance translators of Vitruvius, a Roman author writing about architecture at the time of Emperor Augustus. What emerged from these translations, and further theorising was that the physical space within buildings acquired a symbolic significance via the , "… Order…Arrangement…Proportion, Symmetry, Propiety and Economy… of the building itself. As Vitruvius himself pointed out,

"The planning of Temples depends on symmetry: architects must diligently understand the methods of this. It arises from proportion…. Proportion consists in taking a fixed module, in each case, both parts of a building and for the whole, by which the method of symmetry is put into practice. For without symmetry and proportion no temple can have a regular plan; that is it must have an exact proportion worked out after the fashion of the members of a well-shaped body…In like fashion the members of temples ought to have dimensions of their several parts answering suitably to the general sum of their magnitude…. If a man lies on his back with his hands and feet outspread, and the centre of a circle is located in his navel, then his hands and feet will touch the circumference: a square can also be produced in the same way … the height of a body from the sole of the foot to the crown of the head equal to the span of the outstretched arms."

Hence the proportions of the human form became the proportions for buildings, establishing an aesthetic rooted in the idea of man being the measure of everything. The proportion of columns taken from the proportions of a mans legs, and the spaces between the parts of buildings based on the proportions of other parts of the human body. The logic of this was underwritten by the appeal to a belief in harmony, the basis of which could be discovered through arithmetic and geometry, as suggested by Pythagoras in the intervals of sound- the proportions of vibrating strings and their sound being- 1 to 2= octave, 2 to 3 = fifth, 3 to 4 = fourth. Plato in the Timaeus also points to the idea of harmony in numbers, in doubling or trebling, and these ideas fed the search for principles applied by Renaissance architects, and other artists. More generally Western Philosophy, certainly from Plato onwards, was also engaged in this search for coherence between inner and outer worlds, with ideas flowing between all branches of thought and practice, and between the physical and the metaphysical, the technical and the poetic.

The search for the location of the soul was no small matter, but influenced the shape of the physical world, and the internal landscape of human minds. For the spaces enclosed by Renaissance architects were never merely empty space, but contained both physical and spiritual energy, which resonate with our own internal spaces, which also contain their own physical and spiritual energy. And hence the wind in our lungs is much more than just air, but the breath of life, and the small ventricles of our brains, no mere cavities but vast temples for the residence of souls.

Canto X

ONE OF THE practices among the wealthy Greco-Roman families occupying Egypt during Roman rule was to affix portraits of the deceased to the top cover of their burial caskets. Many of these portraits have survived, and rather than glorifying death by presenting the person as sleeping, the portraits vividly depict them in the fullness of life. There is an eeriness to the modern mind about these life-like portraits, partly because it is possible to imagine the deceased having the portrait prepared perhaps many years before their death, and like a doppelganger displayed in full view, occupying its own place in the house, perhaps as a memento- mori, its image untouched by time, while its owner`s face gradually submitted to the ravages of aging and time Another reason we find these portraits disturbing is the contradiction between the external image, of someone alive on the face of the coffin, and the lifeless body within. It seems to us that the notion of souls and bodies, of interior life and exterior appearance has been reversed, and the categories confused.

But what is most intriguing about these portraits is their realism; many of them have a photographic quality suggested by the liveliness of the eyes, created by two minute specks of white painted on the pupils of the eye, giving the eye a life-like lustre, and giving life to the whole portrait. What in fact these two small white dots create is a believable presence of life, and perhaps it is this sense of `presence`, our unconscious awareness of our own presence, and that of others, which more than anything else communicates to us our sense of Being.

The various ways in which we use the word presence suggests that there is substantiality about someone or something. We speak of presence of mind, meaning that we are in touch with reality, and in the theatre we describe some actors as possessing `stage presence`, meaning that their performance is believably real, and in the field of Hi-Fi sound systems, manufacturers claim that their `speakers` have `presence`, that is that the reproduction of sound is authentic, realistic, alive! And yet the idea of `presence`, rather than being central to our understanding of consciousness, is peripheral; at best simply ignored , or at worst rejected as archaic and meaningless because it resonates loosely with something intangible, and immeasurable. Even in the specialised field of human growth and development, where it might be reasoned that the onset of self-awareness and the awareness of others, so vital to our social functioning, is not on the list of any developmental scales used for the assessment of infants. Because within the framework of our current Weltanschauung, we seek to understand objectively rather subjectively, having already almost lost contact with our inner selves.

Yet evidence abounds from many sources, besides that of our own personal experience, that young babies have an uncanny sense of themselves and of others, even though we might stand silently out of sight. It is this awareness, this sixth sense, that has been described by Rupert Shelden , in some situations as a sense of being stared at, that we glean something about the nature of `presence`. But our sensitivity and responsiveness to presence is more than this, more than just physically responding to external physical stimuli. Perhaps this is part of the problem, part of our difficulty in dealing with our sense of presence, because one of our modern-day general assumptions about the physicality of existence, with its taken for granted emphasis on the material and the concrete, is that we interpret experience of ourselves and others almost totally in physical terms. Any other sensing which might occur, usually in the form of feelings of uneasiness, are dismissed as inexplicable. And yet while these intuitions continue to invade our thoughts, we try to reject or bypass them either as meaningless, because they cannot be verified, or as mild forms of disordered thinking.

But it has not always been like this, we know for example that pre-enlightenment thinking was sensitive to the presence of self and others in a very different way, in fact the focus of Elizabethan writing is almost entirely about presence, with an awareness that went beyond the immediate and the mundanely obvious, to that which constituted the real person, their soul. And it is this focus which gives their writing and their analysis of human experience a clarity that we have since lost. In Shakespeare's plays, for example, we come to understand the characters from deep within their soul, a point endorsed by all of the metaphysical poets of that time, especially Donne, who viewed human affection as being essentially a relationship between souls, but necessarily expressed physically through the body.

The general acceptance that individuals possessed presence, both physically and metaphysically, was a taken for granted assumption, but it also had legal implications. Elizabeth's father, Henry the VIII, had formulated the doctrine of the King's Two bodies; a physical body bounded by time and space, and a theological body, which was deemed to be present in every court in the land, dispensing the King's justice. A belief we still give some nodding acceptance to despite our ignorance of its origins. This extension of the notion of `presence` to a symbolic dimension, was part of a comprehensive world-view which was broader, and therefore richer than our present day view of reality. Presence had a universal validity, everyone had presence, even the dead had a tangible presence which we would find frightening, rather than comforting, for it was the existence of presence which was taken as evidence of an interior essence, a person's soul. All of the literary references to the loss of one's shadow, or the lack of one's body smell, are metaphors for the loss of presence, the lack of presence simply meaning ceasing to exist. In our modern world our notions of presence have become diluted and distorted, reduced and dangerously invisible. We have acquired the ability to deny presence to the point of extinction, and have lost the joys of sanctity afforded by one soul to the presence of another.

Canto XI

LANGUAGE IS A slippery device and our biggest problem with it is finding the right words to express exactly what we mean. In everyday interactions the majority of us get by with approximations and clichéd prompts, but when we need to be more precise we use specific terminology. And even then it is still possible for some of our intended meaning to slip through the mesh of our words. Language is not a closed system, far from it, for a single concept may have connotations which are expandable to become a whole history of a particular way of thinking, even of an entire culture, such is the concept - soul.

Cultural theories attempt to identify the origins of such concepts in the; processes, mechanisms and forces underlying the dynamics of a culture, by identifying the core assumptions and beliefs, and the hopes and dreams of a people which are embedded in cultural myths, which are rarely explicitly stated as such, but are embedded as fragments in every-day conversations and utterances. Consequently cultural myths are never static, but constantly open to revision, and as languages change, the underpinning cultural scaffolding of particular concepts is weakened. Meaning shifts, and concepts such as −soul, while appearing to retain cultural value, is reduced to a microscopic fragment of an idea and explanation that that previously stood at the heart of many civilisations, such is the fate of soul.

This is, after all the twenty-first century, and the thoughts that fill our heads now are grounded in a concrete reality, the modern view is that there is non other! These thoughts can be shaped, and cast and chiselled, so to speak with real hands, and not conjured out of thin air like some miasmic mist from which demons and sprites emerge. While modern men seek to understand and explain any remaining mysteries, winkling them out of the tiniest recesses; any hint of anything mysterious which might remain and which cannot be accounted for brings a kind of paralysis, in the form of the darkest thunder-clouds of doubt. They come rumbling out of nowhere-threatening an intellectual storm or flooding rain. The echoing thunder speaks to their sense of logic that shapes their ideas which are like dark clouds floating across their horizons- their formations pursuing our deadened imaginations like ghosts of ancient hunters and shaman. Understandably, if questioned, these modern thinkers would deny any possibility of any significance in any of this; after all, how can the shape of clouds signify anything? But the wicked thing about language is that words beget images some of which attach themselves to random thoughts, and unprocessed thoughts become worms in ripe fruit of the imagination.

This process of changing world views, which in conjunction with the reworking of etymology, fundamentally changes the nature of human relationships, including our relationship with ourselves. In the name of `modern` efficiency everyman has learned to communicate in sound bites, to be informed by and carried easily by e-mail and mobile phone text; consequently the family-tree of ideas and sentiments that hang on each and every concept is reduced to a one dimensional meaning in our one- size-fits- all culture. The modern mind cannot tolerate too much richness of thought; most of what has been written in the past is now incomprehensible. It is ironic, that at this time in human history, the so-called "linguistic turn" which describes the hegemony of language in almost every field of modern living, common-usage is reduced to a mere mumble, including our descriptions of ourselves. Perhaps it is part of the general `dumbing down which is fast becoming the lingua franca of modern global culture. A culture-lite which embraces the lowest common denominator in wit and wisdom and raises them up as exemplary individuals, to be worshiped as `Celebrities` to be worshipped and imitated by the common herd.

What needs for education, what needs for thought, and what needs for beauty? The restricted limits of our language, to paraphrase Wittgenstein, mean the restricted limits of our world! And if our present world is so diminished, how can we even begin to think about the next? The `expressive` has been eroded at the expense of the technical; technical clichés and techno-babble have become essential parts of modern ego-self-defensiveness. In every-day conversations words have become detached from the concepts they attempt to communicate. Now, words, to paraphrase again, this time Humpty Dumpty, mean whatever we want them to mean. In other words, such *words* mean almost nothing.

To ask questions of modern man; would a rose by any other name smell just as sweet, or to compare his lover to a summer's day, or to love to the extent his soul can reach, could he answer ? Perhaps not! Yet there should be awe and beauty even in ultra-modern concepts, for example in quantum theory there is the most amazing idea that `entangled` atoms can communicate with each other even if they are millions of miles apart; the modern mind thinks – faster computers, the `expressive` mind thinks-soul! The modern convergent mind thinks `selves`- as socially constructed ways of describing individual's uniqueness , the `expressive divergent mind thinks –soul, as something more than selves, something profoundly more, and bigger and wider, perhaps a mere word in appearance, but as a concept boundless and immeasurable.

At one time there was a specific language dedicated to the soul which was reflexive and meditative but this has been eroded almost to the point of extinction, and having lost the language we have also lost the means of being in touch with our souls. We are now living in a time when almost everyone in the western world has access to an oracle in the form of the internet. Ask any question and receive sometimes a thousand answers, but if you do not know the purpose of the question, the answers you get will be as ambiguous as those from the ancient Greek Oracles. To enquire about souls; their history, their geography, their existence or their demise, or any other whimsical question would give access to information far beyond that available to previous generations. At the push of a button we can know considerably more about souls than any previous generation, but we cannot experience them!

For previous generations, especially those living before the printing press knowledge and understanding was very much localised, and in the particular case of questions about souls, knowledge was shaped by shared experiences in the community and interpreted within a particular religious framework. For example in rural Europe the idea of the Christian soul generated its own variegated folk lore which extended beyond the theological doctrine of the church, to such matters as; `soul loss`, souls stolen by vampires, souls possessed by demons, souls sold to and bought by the devil! Such ideas and beliefs shaped culture and social behaviour and set the limits on what was morally acceptable. So by the time these ideas become fixed in written form, such as those by Marlow and Shakespeare they were already deeply embedded in every-day common assumptions as part of the way the world works.

The philosophical conundrums which questioned the reality of the soul was a side issue; the preserve of university Dons and philosophers, their interest has been to prod and poke the current ideas of their times and to draw out and transmute and to define the indefinable! In one way or another we learn that it is something through which we are animated, and with which we experience and think and feel and know and sense and love and continue to be beyond physical existence. And that perhaps it is somewhat like music, containing both `sameness` and `otherness`, or like perfume or wine, with it's notes and melodies, eternal and indestructible, transcendent and sublime, the ultimate reservoir of all our hopes and doubts of our own existence. As such it is the cipher for life itself!

In our almost soulless world journalists and writers still hold the word `soul` in reserve when commenting on matters of ultimate human concern, especially when depicting the meaninglessness and emptiness of modern life. And try as they might to deny or hide the roots of their ideas, psychotherapists, teachers and even architects utilise the shadows of half forgotten paradigms in which the notion of soul represented wholeness, human integrity and authenticity. The idea of soul resonates through the rhythms of the profoundest human utterances; it is the X factor which distinguishes the greatest dramatic performances on film and stage, and the distinguishing feature which separates the genuine from the fake in every form of art. To get things going at a `party` it is not enough for someone to be simply the `life` (lively one) of the party; to make it `come alive` it is necessary to become both the life and soul. A phrase everyone knows and understands but mostly unaware of its shamanistic resonances. It is as if modern man walks continually in the shadows. He feels the emptiness and tries to fill it with all the modern substitutes obtainable through virtual media worlds.

Canto XII

LANGUAGE IS FUNDAMENTALLY symbolic and is the currency of everyday social exchange, yet our present-day interest in the nature of language emphasises the cognitive over the expressive, especially in approaches dedicated to its analysis and acquisition. This suggests that we are now more interested in meaning than feelings. Yet the nature of language itself mimics human nature insofar as it has body and soul, a distinction between meaning and interpretation which an over-academicised concern with structure has shifted away from the natural balance between these two; now valuing objectivity over subjectivity. Whereas at other points in our history, our language combined both depth and texture more equitably to the point that its rhythms and subtleties evoked profound and spiritual nuances that modern language lacks. Even the most sensitive modern poetry has difficulty in touching our souls in the way that Shakespeare or Donne were capable of doing. This is not just a complaint about `dumbing down` of language, although that surely is part of the present decline in the quality of human thought and communication, but more the consequence of the shift in meaning of central human concepts such as; sympathy, love, desire, passion. These and other such concepts are shaped in modern consciousness more as a consequence of their commercial connotations than their reference to human emotion.

Passion, for example, with its Classical Greek roots in

(Παθος) pathos, meaning `suffering`, is now associated more with the sensation of eating chocolates rather than some overpowering emotion; such is the persuasive power of commercial advertising! Its general use changing very considerably since its apogee in the seventeenth century, when it was associated with the deepest emotions emanating from the depths of one's being experienced only by the soul. The consequences of demolishing the soul are that a whole landscape of meaning has been dismantled, damaging human self- consciousness more than we realise, by numbing sensitivities of our inner selves. When it was precisely that sensitivity that enabled writers of Shakespeare's time, to quite literally, get to the heart of the matter; because of their tacit understanding of a spiritual core shaping their being.

We get closest to that kind of understanding when we enter the minds of Macbeth or Lear, both driven by prototypical passions we can only vaguely imagine touching our own modern sense of being, because without a soul our understanding of passion is diminished to little more than strong physical feelings, and then only feebly expressed. To Elizabethan writers passion was the lingua franca of the soul, and it was only through the soul that passion could be expressed. John Donne, foremost among the Metaphysical poets, went beyond the world of the senses, seeing the vital core of the human person as composed of three layers of soul; an outer layer being `vegetable` concerned with growth and reproduction, next an animal soul responsible for `sense and movement`, and central to these the human soul, that which is exclusively human and containing divine energy which endows it with immortality. In his *Devotions*

(XVIII), Donne identifies the outer layers of soul as the medium between body and mind, but the innermost core of persons is the *immortall soule*, and it is this alone which expresses passion and is moved by it.

One of the qualities of metaphysical poetry is its open display of erudite learning; Donne and the other Metaphysical poets were fascinated by the complexity of human emotions, especially the more intense passions. It was this over-intellectualised speculation about the nature and composition of this inner core of being, the soul; which later exposed it to scientific ridicule, but the general idea that souls were moved by passion stretches back to the earliest European literature. Each of the Greek gods, for example, was characterised by one of the passions, and although Plato and other philosophers warned against it, passion became a central theme in the development of European thought, and was the driving force behind the early development of Christianity; martyrdom being the ultimate proof of that passion.

Shakespeare was well aware of the close correspondence between sacred and secular passion via the ideas of sacrifice, which still lurks deep within our unconscious. To die voluntarily for one's faith is the strongest evidence of passion, sanctified by the term martyrdom, but to die for the love of another human, carries both censure and admiration. To Shakespeare's original audience, the deaths of Romeo and Juliet must have been terrifyingly blasphemous, as was the passion which much earlier drove Abelard first to seduce Heloise, and to subsequently sustain an undiminished passion, although both living separate lives, for a further thirty years. Abelard`s sacrifice to that passion was castration, after which the two lovers retreated to religious houses, he to become an abbot and Heloise an abbess. From his monks cell he wrote his second letter to Heloise, "You are greater than heaven, greater than the world….". And she replied, "Even during the celebration of the mass, when our prayers should be purer, lewd visions of those pleasures take such a hold upon my unhappy soul ….sometimes my thoughts are betrayed in a movement of my body, or they break out in an unguarded word."

The idea of souls being moved by passion is central to its meaning, as Desdemona reminds Othello, "Some bloody passion shakes your very frame." although we no longer put it that way. Instead we define passion as madness, as obsession, as neurosis; in effect we have almost tamed it to the point that any display of passion is regarded as uncouth and threatening. This fear of passion can be seen as one of the prophetic themes in Orwell`s `Nineteen eighty four` and Huxleys `Brave New World`. In both these novels passion is seen as a threat to society, and has to be controlled. Almost everything issues from this fear of passion, from sexual to political passion, and modern societies seek to provide controlled outlets in various forms of entertainment. For some individuals the adrenalin `rush` will be sought by participating in dangerous adventures, or for the less spirited as spectators of team games, where the social dynamics of large crowds amplify individual emotions to the point of overwhelming passion.

That modern societies take it upon themselves to contain and control passion, whilst at the same time manipulating it in the form of military, political and economic control is evidence of a deep and disturbing ambivalence towards the primitive fear of passion as an expression of something unknown. On the one hand the soul's passion is dismissed as superstition, while on the other it is feared as an all consuming raw energy, capable of swallowing civilisations whole, and reducing everything to their primitive origins. We moderns conjure it into existence through concepts such as Freud's *Id*, or Nietzsche's *Dionysian*, and use these terms as though they will protect us by containing its socially corrosive power. But once out of the crucible, it re-energises the flagging soul, and restores vitality, quickens the pulse, and reignites the will to love.

Canto XIII

CHILDREN'S DOLLS ARE more than mere playthings, more even than pretend babies through which we as children nurture our emotions, but are surrogate vessels for human souls, to act as mediators in the relationship between our material and immaterial selves. And as such they provide, during our childhood, the earliest physical means through which we communicate with our inner-selves, to be replaced as we get older, by other forms of surrogate persons such as; photographs, decorative figurines; sculptures, statues, effigies, and other cultural representations of human persons. This relationship that we Humans have with dolls is an ancient one, dolls being among some of the earliest archaeological artefacts discovered alongside tools and weapons, and existing in all cultures, we have shared our lives with them, metaphorically and sometimes literally since the emergence of consciousness.

As children, through our play we breathe life into them, giving them their souls and identity, which we take for granted as the way the world is. This perhaps is our earliest metaphysical experience, revealing an intuitive knowledge of an inner essence which has agency, for our dolls participate in our daily lives, not as mere material objects, but as other beings, ambiguously similar but different from ourselves. Embodying within them something of our spirit, but also as independent beings with souls of their own, they provide us ambivalently with both a mirror of ourselves, and a companion who knows us as intimately as we know ourselves. And as such they also provide us with our earliest experience of loss and separation, through which we come to glimpse our dark unconscious fears of our own mortality.

There is no generic term to describe the whole range of entities which replicate the human form, but in one way or another we endow them with what we believe to be our essential essence, even to the point of sharing our evolution with them. Either as plaything, companion, sacrificial victim, entertainer, sacred effigy, surrogate offspring, slave, as humanoids, or in one the many other forms required by rituals and other social activities, they have come to occupy the middle ground between inanimate matter and sentient beings. But that middle ground is ambiguous, even when we become mature adults, for our relationship with them offers a particular kind of transference, through which we can become as one them, and they as one of us. Stringed marionettes, ventriloquist dolls, voodoo dolls, and mechanical automata of previous centuries and the present-day humanoid robots, are all manifestations of this transference. In ancient Rome, small figurines represented deceased family members who continued to live in the family home, and who were offered food at meal times and spoken of as full family members.

The life we give them is not fabricated in the form of anything like a `social self`, a mere set of surface characteristics attached to a social identity; it is something deeper than this. For, even as young children we are aware that there are many other dolls identical to our own, in most cases indistinguishable, and owned by other children. But the uniqueness of character we endow, and which is embodied by our own particular doll sets it apart from all others, and it is this quality of its invisible uniqueness, this something like a prototypical idea of a soul, which gives it life. This intuitive awareness that even very young children experience, that their dolls share an inner life similar to their own suggests that a sense of being is innately part of what it is to be human. And that this indefinable something, which the child can grasp and comprehend, but cannot directly express except through an acted-out relationship with the doll, sets the pattern of ambivalence and ambiguity we have with our inner selves, and which remains with us for the rest of our lives. And it is perhaps this ambivalence and ambiguity which we later come to express as enigmatic, which is the deepest source of our uncertainty about who we are; that sense of doubt which we try to balance with our desire for certainty.

Modern children's dolls are designed to eradicate uncertainty; they are now provided mechanically with their own voice and character, removing the opportunity and imaginative effort from children to imbue their own dolls with soul, and consequently to close off early in their lives an opportunity to engage themselves Instead what the modern child has is a manufactured item, a product which exemplifies perfectly our disenchanted material world, where science and technology has come to replace the mysterium of an internal world, and has literally turned the inside world out. Dolls have left the world of childhood to become machines, soulless workers whose employment is the repetitive manufacturing tasks which require precision and replication. And it is within this soulless universe that designers and technicians compete with one another to build humanoid robots more human than themselves, to build and give life to robots with souls and feelings.

Canto XIV

NIETZSCHE'S THEORY OF eternal recurrence has resonances with Bergsons and Jung`s ideas about `time`, that is that each moment contains much more than what is actually happening at that particular moment. In fact it suggests that each moment contains the echoes of what has already happened to us and to the whole of humanity since the beginning of time, and that is why sometimes we have the sense of deja vue.

The earliest echoes perhaps are from the caves of our ancestors which contain the earliest signs of man's spirituality. The most haunting figure in which we can identify this spark of spirituality, as something belonging to ourselves, is the dancing figure, with an appearance part human and part animal, in the Volp Caves at Les Trois Freres. This figure, painted around 14, 000 years ago, is particularly intriguing because it is completely unlike any other cave images anywhere, yet we know instinctively as we view it, despite its ambiguity that it is a man disguised as an animal, wearing antlers, and not just walking or standing, but dancing. This almost certainly is the first shaman, declaring that shamanism is the birth of our sense of the transcendent.

It is uncanny then, that centuries later Plato should depict the birth of rational thought as moving out of the shadows of the cave, and subsequently that caves should become a metaphor for ignorance and stupidity. Yet in countless anthropological studies caves are depicted as wombs, as thresholds marking the transition between one kind of space and another. They are more than mere holes in the ground, for the early Greeks they were the entrance to the underworld, the place inhabited by souls; and by extension both oracles and amphitheatres share something of this cave-like mysterious power, which were the means through which humans communicated with their extended selves. Not surprisingly these holes in the ground are almost universally sacred in some context, for example, to the ancient Anasazi people at Pueblo Bonito in New Mexico, the carefully stone-built entrances to their caves (kiva), represent the birth-holes through which the first people emerged in their creation myths, which also explains why the most common form of human burial is to return the dead to the belly of the earth, either in caves, catacombs or graves. Even the great tombs of the Graeco-Roman world, the Viking burial chambers, Celtic graves in Ireland and Scotland, the Pyramids, the ancient Chinese tombs of Zhongshan, and the burial pits at Sanxingdui, all of these and many more, are different forms of the archetypal cave. In literature too the cave is identified as the most mysterious of places. For Coleridge it is the site where Alph, the sacred river runs, and for Forster, in `Passage to India`, it provides the space for the echo in the Marabar caves, an echo which divides Eastern spirituality from Western rationality, a place that reduces everything to the same noise!

"They are dark caves. Even when they open towards the sun, very little light penetrates down the entrance tunnel into the circular chamber. There is little to see, and no eye to see it , until the visitor arrives for his five minutes, and strikes a match. Immediately another flame rises in the depths of the rock and moves towards the surface like an imprisoned spirit; the walls of the chamber have been most marvellously polished. The two flames approach and strive to unite, but cannot, because one of them breathes air, the other stone. A mirror inlaid with lovely colours divides the lovers, delicate stars of pink and grey interpose, exquisite nebulae, shadings fainter than the tail of a comet or the midday moon, all evanescent life of granite, only here visible. Fists and fingers thrust above the advancing soil - here at last is their skin, finer than any covering acquired by the animals, smoother than windless water, more voluptuous than love. The radiance increases, the flames touch one another, kiss, expire. The cave is dark again, like all caves."

But the ultimate image of the cave in Western culture is Christ's tomb, the place where spirit triumphs over the material body, as the definitive event which characterises western consciousness and the nature of transcendence.

Canto XV

FORTY YEARS AGO astronomers investigating the origins of the universe heard a noise on a radio telescope that convinced them that they were hearing the echo of the so-called Big Bang that had occurred fourteen billion years earlier. They described the noise as sounding like a distant hum, a ghostly remnant of the reverberations of the beginning of time. This particular echo continues to resonate through the whole of space as a haunting reminder of the moment when time and space began, and perhaps will continue to reverberate until the end of time and possibly after when all that will be left will be that echo.

On a much smaller time scale, perhaps a mere thirty thousand years ago, cave dwellers responded to a different echo, the echoes of their own voices and movements which could quite possibly have been the first stimulus to the idea that we are more than simply our bodies. We know that during this time, during the Upper Palaeolithic period, Homo sapiens emerged with a different level of consciousness to the Neanderthals, and with an awareness that later led to an array of complex behaviours. The echoes they heard and responded to were of equivalent importance to our species as the big bang was to the whole of our universe.

Those first echoes in the caves were the very beginning of mankind's relationship with his soul. Not only in the sense that he had discovered something about himself, about his inner voice, but also that these reverberations and resonances put him in touch with another dimension beyond that which was familiar to him. In modern terms, the psychoacoustic influences of the echoing environment had altered his state of consciousness. Recent research has shown that particular locations within caves resonate in response to particular notes which can affect the central nervous system, and which can induce a range of feelings including feelings of dread and *ekstasis*, the sensation of `stepping out` of one's self.

These echoes were a vital part of human evolution, and would have stimulated the early inhabitants in several ways. Almost certainly many of the early cave occupants would have spent long periods, perhaps several days in the dark caverns, with only small fires for illumination. Under these circumstances serotonin levels would have been low which would have had a depressing effect on their moods. But against this the psychoacoustic effects of the echoes, with their continuous resonances and reverberations would have stimulated their brain's reward system, as well as releasing brain hormones oxytocin, and vasopressin, which are known to stimulate bonding behaviours, there were also opiods (pleasure hormones) which would have induced feelings of elation. Almost certainly there would have been some particular individual cave-dwellers who were sufficiently stimulated, and who were sometimes in ecstatic and euphoric states, who not only tried to express their exaggerated moods in their cave paintings and decorations and by dancing and producing musical sounds from primitive instruments, but would most likely have also developed nurturing behaviours directed towards other group members.

While there is no way of absolutely knowing how this would have worked, but it is reasonable to draw on our modern insights about how human development and behaviour operates. Possibly some individuals with particular genetic predispositions would have been more responsive to the caves` psychoacoustic stimuli; we know for example that there are certain genes, for example one identified as VMAT2 which can predispose carriers to feelings of transcendence. Most probably they would have become addicted to these euphoric highs, and their new sensitivities would also have set them apart from the rest of their group as being recognisably more socially responsive and compassionate, and more capable and competent, especially in response to others in their communities who were distressed. The conclusions we might draw from all of the evidence and the discussions surrounding the activities of our ancestors` experiences in caves suggests that around this time there was a shift in consciousness and a new repertoire of feelings which included; a sense of awe and mystery, compassion, empathy, love, and fascination, all of which were to become part of a new sense of being.

This new sense of `Being` profoundly affected the direction of human evolution because it shifted human consciousness to a new level of reflexivity which included intuitions of an inner life, and an intuition or conviction perhaps that this `inner life` extended beyond any basic innate nurturing instincts, beyond that which even other animals have, to a higher level of articulation; in a word, they had discovered the capacity to love. And it is this capacity to love, with its *psychic dimension* which includes empathy and compassion that specifically identifies us as human, and which, as Erich Fromm has pointed out.

"..is not primarily a relationship to a specific person; (but) it is an *attitude* ,an *orientation of character* which determines the relatedness of a person to the world as a whole, not towards one `object` of love."

And so` love` became the basis for a completely new ontology.

"The most fundamental kind of love, which underlies all types of love is *brotherly love*. By this I mean the sense of responsibility, care, respect, knowledge of any other human being, the wish to further his life. This is the kind of love the Bible speaks of when it says: love thy neighbour as thyself. Brotherly love is love for all human beings; it is characterised by its lack of exclusivity."

Most academic considerations of the nature of love make distinctions along a continuum from eros to agape, and then continue to dissect it until it becomes incomprehensible. Erich Fromm`s point is that Love as an *orientation of character*, is fundamentally the defining characteristic of being human, and that whatever form it takes, either towards one individual or more generally towards humanity, it is basically the same thing. In fact it is often impossible to analyse the various qualities of love that individuals experience because the very concept of love is as diaphanous as that of the soul. And while we experience very complex feelings and sensations which we associate with loving, when we try to define them we reach a point beyond rational explanation, beyond the physical, emotional, psychological, etc. All that we can do then is to admit that we cannot explain it or locate it, because while the experience seems to be highly personal, in fact what we are doing is tapping into a vast reservoir of psychic energy; familial, communal, social, and universal, all at the same time. And at some point whilst we are thinking about this, the boundaries become blurred and we become confused, similar to the philosophical confusion concerning individual souls and world soul. But for our ancestors in the caves, most probably there would have been no confusion, but simply a new intuition that a sense of belonging to their group was a vital source of contentment and wellbeing.

What is meant by 'love' as an *orientation of character* goes far deeper than we can at first imagine, for orientation is essentially direction, and Fromm intends by this a massive change in direction. This crucial shift in consciousness which occurred during this relatively brief period of evolutionary time, when some of our ancestors inhabited the cavernous interiors of the earth, and with whatever combined effects of their environment, somehow they emerged with a new personal and social impulse, an imperative to reach out to one another, to connect, if not to understand, but to respond, and sympathise and empathise in any way that found deeper roots than the merely physical. How else can we characterise this other than to admit to a spiritual dimension.

What followed from this `spiritual emergence`, as part of the package so to speak, as part of this new mind-set was the constant urge to comprehend it, which we might understand as the beginning of culture. For the urge to seek meaning, to yearn to connect cause and effect, to raise the question *why*, which goes way beyond the merely ordinary *how* ? Almost certainly this is how the sense of the inner-life began, rather than through some circuitous religious quest. Surely the outward journey came after the journey inward! For this essentially is the Human Paradox, man's search for an understanding of himself, for the essence of his being. His search for a soul is not a modern phenomenon but an integral part of his humanity. And surprisingly although we think of ourselves as being out of the cave, having left it millennia hence, we somehow return to the cave in one way or another. In this sense the cave is both a metaphor and a reality for the emergence of the soul.

Love as an orientation signifies something extraordinary. We know that all animals show affection towards their own and sometimes other species, but love is more than affection, more than emotion, more than physical response, although these can be part of it. Love is the means through which we connect with everything, from our own sense of self to those who are closest and beyond, to the whole of humanity, the environment, the universe, the past the present and the future. Love is extensive throughout the whole chain of being. It is the social and spiritual glue that holds us all together; it is the energy that substantiates our existence

While the multiplicity of meanings associated with love stretches the concept beyond any graspable definition, the mere fact that it has become so extended and inclusive indicates our human yearning to claim it as part of ourselves and as part of our lives. In short, to be able to feel loved and capable of loving is acknowledged as essential to `normal` life, which includes knowing that we belong to others, and having a place in the order of things; of membership, of having value and recognition as one of many but also unique and irreplaceable, as real and authentic.

All of these attributes somehow coalesce as a consequence of the shift in consciousness and significantly severed the link between us as a species and our nearest non-human cousins. Perhaps it is this cluster of needs for connectedness with other humans; with individuals, with groups, with our tribe, the whole of our species which we translate into `soul`, as the distinguishing feature which characterises our humanness.

Canto XVI

IN THE MAHABHARATA, the ancient Hindu poem of more than a hundred thousand stanzas long, the human soul is depicted as fragments belonging to a universal soul, a kind of super soul which energises and sustains all living things. Hence humans are part of a great chain of being connecting the whole of creation, in which this relationship is acknowledged as necessary to the well-being of both.

This forgotten or suppressed ancient wisdom has re-emerged as ecopsychology, a combination of ecology and psychology, which draws on insights drawn from both our external and internal worlds; both the psychological and the physical, and connecting our internal and external landscapes, and so restoring the balance between our sense of being and the world`s ecology, fusing our private soul with anima mundi-the soul of the world. It is within this deeply rooted reciprocal relationship that we rediscover the source of our well-being, physically, mentally and spiritually, and to break this connection is to damage both ourselves and the natural world.

Relocating ourselves within nature is fundamental to understanding ecology, but ecopsychology goes further, seeing ecological health of the planet as directly related to the mental health of its inhabitants because the human soul is embedded in the vital forces which power nature. Mainstream psychology depicts mental illness as caused by disconnectedness in some significant way, disconnected from others and disconnected from ourselves. The vital point being our relationship with ourselves, but ecopsychology shifts the focus to our relationship with nature which is fundamentally deeper, and that as urbanised beings we are grieving for our dying planet while we continue to exploit and destroy its subtle ecology. Our alienation is all the more painful because it is the result of our own selfishness and greed.

In ecopsychology the spiritual dimension confronts the material directly by examining the ecological consequences of our social, political and economic behaviour. Our bad relationship with nature is a direct consequence of our materialistic values, emphasising our need to have rather than our desire to be. It is becoming clearer as globalisation continues that it is our relationship with nature which is the fundamental internal contradiction of capitalism. The cultural consequences of advanced capitalism is to reduce all value to profit and wealth, and western cultures which promote the pursuit of wealth above everything else not only controls the mechanisms by which wealth is created and distributed, but it also controls the mechanisms of mass communication through which its values are transmitted. Against this relentless capitalistic tide which drives consumerism and the acquisition of wealth an ecopsychological counter-culture is a very small voice, but it is an internal voice, a small clear voice which speaks to the soul, and its presence is the tormentor of our sanity.

Canto XVII

To **WHAT EXTENT** any writer speaks for his age is questionable. Certainly in the past when there were fewer books this might have been possible, but now that shared consciousness is mediated through so many outlets it is not so clear how an idea originates, or is shaped ,or is finally absorbed, or to what effect! All that we can know at an individual personal level is that from time to time there is a shift in our own consciousness, and perhaps of a few others we share our lives with. Yet despite the increased range of media, and the rapid flow of news and other information, there are some modern authors who have come to be recognised as capturing the essence of their times. Sometimes these have been prophetic as in Orwell's Nineteen Eighty Four and Aldus Huxley's Brave New World, while at other times more prosaic, capturing the spirit of a milieu; but even more than this, finding the words and fastening the images which speak of the hopes and fears of a kind of collective consciousness, for a particular moment in time. For example as in Forster`s "Passage to India" and Joseph Heller`s "Catch Twenty Two". While neither of these novels was intentionally a comment on the status of the human soul, their obliqueness to that hidden dimension is more penetrating for being so. Who for example can forget Miss Quested`s encounter with the echo, " ...a terrifying echo" in the Marabar caves, or the absurdity of a self-contradicting rule in "Catch -22"?

Whereas for Forster numinousity shines through all the dirt and debris of human intrigues despite the attempts to "ravish the unknown" through the pursuit of rational thinking, while for Heller the rational ultimately becomes nonsense. A kind of nonsense which finally leads to despair as Captain Yossarian, the bombardier tries to comfort Snowdon, the dying tail gunner as they return from a bombing raid. Joseph Heller captures the complex mixture of absurdity, anarchy, and moral outrage, as Yossarian tends the dying Snowdon.

" `I`m cold,` Snowdon said softly. `I`m cold.`
`You`re going to be all right, kid,` Yossarian reassured him with a grin. `Your going to be all right.`
`I`m cold,` Snowden said again in a frail, childlike voice. I`m cold`.
`There , there,` Yossarian said, because he did not know what else to say. `There, there.`
Yossarian attends to one wound, but then discovers another, this time," A chunk of flak more than three inches big had shot into his other side just underneath the arm and blasted all the way through, drawing whole mottled quarts of Snowden along with it through the gigantic hole in his ribs it made as it blasted out. Yossarian screamed a second time and squeezed both hands over his eyes. His teeth were chattering in horror. He forced himself to look again. Here was God's plenty, all right, he thought bitterly as he stared - liver, lungs, kidneys, ribs, stomach and bits of the stewed tomatoes Snowden had eaten that day for lunch.
" …`I`m cold,`Snowden whimpered .`I`m cold.`

`There, there,` Yossarian mumbled mechanically in a voice too low to be heard.`There, there.`

Yossarian was cold, too, and shivering uncontrollably. He felt goose pimples clacking all over him as he gazed down despondently at the grim secret Snowden had spilled all over the messy floor. It was easy to read the message in his entrails. Man was matter, that was Snowden`s secret. Drop him out a window and he'll fall. Set fire to him and he`ll burn. Bury him and he`ll rot, like any other garbage. The spirit gone, man is garbage. That was Snowden`s secret. Ripeness was all.

Canto XVIII

HISTORICALLY THE MIDDLE Ages were the hey-day for the European Soul. Life for the ordinary citizen was harsh and perilous, with the focus of fear on sudden death. Against this background of physical threat there was the hope of spiritual continuity in the survival of the soul, but this required faith, prayer and religious conformity. For each town and village the local church provided comfort and control. For a largely illiterate peasant population sermons were not enough. In the early Middle Ages colourful wall paintings in rural churches began appearing across the whole of Europe, and continued to be popular for more than five hundred years. They were crude and primitive in style, but they served their purpose of communicating rather than decorating, and their central message was the constant reminder; ` Care for your Soul ` One favourite theme of these paintings was the final judgement at the end of time, depicting Christ in Glory at the Second Coming, usually depicted with scenes of Doom and the Apocalypse in the form of four ghostly horsemen.

It is almost impossible to imagine the impact these gruesome images would have had on individuals and populations whose gaze took in these messages and their meaning, but it must have been immense, for every single soul was required to attend church every Sunday, to be always confronted and threatened by these images. Which means that for more than five centuries all the eyes of Europe would have perused and absorbed these images and contemplated their consequences.

It is easy for us to dismiss these wall paintings as allegorical, but during the same period in which they became popular the whole of Europe was prone to regular devastating famines with universal crop failure frequently accompanied by widespread plagues. During the Black Death in 1349 for example, more than twenty million people died in Europe, which was one third of the population. In some places the death rate was even higher, reason enough to trust and fear the terrifying and threatening veracity of the wall-painting's message. Folk memories of these images and their physical manifestations were so deeply etched into medieval consciousness that subsequent attempts to destroy them did little to diminish their power and influence. Even after the Reformation and the destruction of many of these church images, the four horsemen of the apocalypse still symbolised the end of the world in the form of etchings and drawings.

Even today when modern film-makers and illustrators use these archetypal images to tap into our deepest unconscious, it is impossible for us to sense the sheer terror these pictures must have invoked because modern humans are no longer afraid of the dark in quite the same way! But for the mediaeval man these images fitted the times and his tempo of life. He knew that Death, War, Famine and Plague would come speedily mounted on fierce steeds and with such ferocity that nobody would have time to run or hide or do anything to redeem their soul.

Our fears of this kind of terror lingers still in our unconscious minds, but is now transformed and sublimated beneath layers of sanitised messages and impressions which shield and distance us from the most primitive of these threats. We reason that Famine and Plague belong to other times and other places, as do souls, because modern consciousness has relegated them to a semi-fictional realm, but the shadows of the horsemen still stalk us, not in the scarcity of food but in its plenitude.

If we were to revise our apocalyptic fears symbolically we would replace the redundant four horsemen with just one singular over-weight rider mounted on a ridiculously over-weight old nag and his name would be "Excess". This modern bringer of death ironically is not starvation and famine, but gluttony and greed in its most physical manifestation: over-consuming. Not only do we eat too much, we feel pressed to purchase more than we could possibly consume, and we waste more than six billion pounds worth of what we cannot eat annually. The reasons for this obsession with consumption runs deeper than simplistic neurotic needs for food per se. Certainly eating disorders and comfort eating explain some of the drives to this form of self-destruction, but obesity and other over-weight related conditions have already reached epidemic levels throughout the whole western world that we suspect that its cause must run deeper than we can bear to accept.

The need to produce and consume has become a national sickness, and is as much a psychological, social and economic problem as it is a biological one. Yet despite the continuous attention to the serious health dangers of obesity, individuals seem helpless to control their appetites and any resistance to their internal demands to consume, despite the fears, is vanquished by the lure of cheap `bargain` foods from fast-food outlets and supermarkets. The voice of advertising has become more persuasive than that of our own individual consciences! Against the combined buying power of the Supermarkets and their virtual monopolistic control of food production and their relentless mass marketing of food, the modern individual is defenceless.

Supermarkets are more than mere food shops; they have purposely developed a friendly and relaxing atmosphere designed to elevate the simple activity of food-shopping to an emotionally satisfying experience. There is method and magic in the way their wares are displayed to entice and seduce customers to buy more, to ease out of each pocket that little extra that in the long run will boost their profits. In return the loyal customer will be rewarded with points and promises of better value for money.

Supermarket food is mass produced for mass consumption, their operational model mimics the processes of factory farming, their checkouts bearing an uncanny resemblance to the lines of caged factory-farmed chickens, it is all too easy to extrapolate further down the feeding chain to their customer`s consuming habits, consuming the maximum food for the minimum costs.

Ken Evans

But EXCESS, the one remaining horseman of the apocalypse is in no hurry, he can take his time because his victims have neither the energy nor desire to run away. For they no longer have the power to resist; their consuming habits have become an addiction, almost their total reason for existing. The flesh is weak but their spirit, which at one time might have been strong, is now flaccidly impotent. Thankfully there is no need to advertise this in anyway, or to paint these images on walls, for each one is etched a million times on the vacant space left by their departed souls.

Canto XIX

IN MY LOCAL bookstore, situated between Philosophy and Science, there is a tantalising display of books with weird titles. One which constantly catches my eye has the provocative title of something like, `Chicken Soup for the Soul`; it always stares me in the face, sometimes seductively, but I never have time to peep inside, so I have no way of knowing if it hints at the real cost of chicken soup. I have some ideas about souls, and if chicken soup really has soothing properties for such, then no price would be too high. But price and cost, as any entrepreneur will tell you, is not the same thing, and anyway the true cost of anything cannot be calculated simply in terms of money, especially when it comes to chicken soup.

As Mrs Beeton might have said, first take your chicken, which for most of us means from the supermarket. While for us customers this might be frozen chicken in one of its many forms, yet for the supermarket tribe, whatever its shape, it will be described merely as a `product`, which arrives at the rear of the building in a refrigerated truck from a depot somewhere far away, whenever stocks get low. Beyond that, no one gives a dam, them of the supermarket tribe, or us. After all chicken is one product among many, which would have achieved its anonymous status as product before it was even hatched. Sadly, in such a crowded world of supermarkets and chicken farms there is no time to consider the convoluted route from hatchery to dispatchery. From beginning to end, the route and adventures of the chicken, as product, is part of a system, which includes us, the customer, and the many hands through which the chicken must pass before it can hope to sooth souls.

The system, known as globalisation, makes it necessary to regard everything as `product`, and because of the massive scale at which the system works, every participant shares in the anonymity of the product: farmers become producers, factory owners- processors, supermarket chains- retailers, and customers - consumers, all connected, as Marx would say, via the cash nexus. That is the connection and the only connection recognised by the system. But beyond the depot, beyond the horizon the biography of the chicken is embedded in a process that transforms flesh and blood into hard cash, and at every minute stage of that processes a means of adding value.

Globalisation has a mixed reputation; still sometimes confused with the benign idea of a `global village` or `one world`, but Globalisation, `the real thing`, has one aim, to reduce all human interactions to the logic of the market place. Rather than drawing peoples together it does the opposite, because part of its logic, the logic of greed requires the maximum separation possible; geographically, ethnically, nationally, and emotionally. It is this requirement to separate, to interrupt the normal flow of social relationships, which identifies globalisation as sinister.

An essential part of its processes includes severe restrictions on the flow of information about how it goes about its business, which in a world where there is already a surfeit of information about almost everything else, this means in effect that it is able to flourish without serious opposition. For as long as customers continue to purchase their products at prices they are happy with, the logic goes, there are no other questions worth asking. It would perhaps make little difference anyway, even if consumers in the UK discovered how profits were made, or that farmers who had tended and nurtured their chicken, received as little as 2% of the supermarkets asking price, it is unlikely to deter them from further shopping at that particular store, such is the invisible and deadening power of alienation.

The logic of the market demands that both ends of the supply chain are controlled with military efficiency, and sometimes actually using the military and state controls if necessary. For the global markets are far more than national markets writ large, they are part of an agenda set by a new breed of international capitalists, and that agenda requires political, social and psychological control of every individual on the planet. Global systems requires a reorganisation of regions and nations, it defines where in the world products are produced, where they are processed, transported, distributed, and where they are consumed. Rather than being an `open` market, it contrives to become a totally closed system, where for example, producers such as poor South American chicken farmers, have no choice but to sell to the processing and packaging companies, at the owners fixed price, and their specification, their time schedules, etc. The logic of the global market place cascades down through every level of social organisation, from nation to region, down to each individual abode. Consequently, a change in taste leading to changes in patterns of consumption at one part of the planet will have devastating consequences at some other location.

In the case of chickens and similar commodities there is fierce competition to sell to European markets, and so in some South American and South East Asian countries, entire regions are given over to chicken farming. Sometimes the farmers produce a surplus they cannot sell. While the European supermarket price wars impact back through the system, back to the individual producer who is forced to compete with his immediate neighbours, exerting pressures to produce improved products at reduced prices. These economic pressures impact on individuals and communities, causing local and regional cultures and traditions to collapse, to be replaced by foreign values and false cultures.

In both South East Asia and South America indigenous cultures with their traditional value systems have been eroded through the penetration of multinational capitalism. Besides extending markets for the consumption of Western commodities, they have become the new industrial zones based on cheap labour. As producers and consumers they stoke the furnaces of Western materialism, and absorb the overflow of over-produced Western goodies; fast foods, designer clothes, pop music, redundant television series, previous- generation white goods, and misunderstood western values. It is through this process of cultural erosion that personal identity becomes fragmented and detached from indigenous references. In such places where personal selves are socially constructed on the basis of rejecting previous social values, and dependent on the ability to purchase the new self-defining consumer products, the consequences are anomie on a massive scale. This in turn provides the real incentive to consume, and the final triumph of global capitalism, which implies that in order to exist it is necessary to consume.

Any complete examination of Globalisation would necessarily include; economic, political, and sociological analysis, but these in themselves are inadequate, for they fail to capture the extent of human despair. And even psychology and anthropology, which we might expect to probe deeper,fail to explain the personal circumstances of the `common man`. It is an embarrassing point of interest, that whatever else any consideration of Globalisation shows us, we are faced with the realisation that there is no human or social sciences sharp enough to explain the mechanisms of the destruction of the human person.

We think we comprehend the processes of Globalisation, and even understand its components, and its ideology of cultural reductionism, but while attending to what we might think is the whole picture, we ignore the consequences of personal disorder, which underpins the whole enterprise. While both producers and consumers are cynically alienated through the cash nexus, by the Capitalist's naked pursuit of wealth and power, their alienation is not equal. For the consumer participates in that greed through their (contrived) demand for lower prices, which are never at the expense of reduced Corporate profits, but through the deflated value of raw materials and unprocessed products. In effect, we in the West have become the camp guards, maintaining control of the disinherited prisoners of the new economic world order Gulags. Their exclusion tears the souls out of anyone who might have given a dam, and had a yearning for chicken soup.

Canto XX

THERE IS AN interesting problem pertaining to copyright in photography which is perhaps unique to that activity, and which centres on the question of whose finger is on the button. Apparently the ownership of the camera and other equipment is irrelevant, or even who selects the camera settings and frames the picture, despite all of this the copyright of the picture belongs to the owner of the finger on the shutter button!

The unfairness of this revolves around the central question of the creator of the picture, and creation is surely an act of the imagination, the ability to imagine the composition of a photograph, rather than the pressing of a mere button.

Despite being the subject of John Lennon's most famous song it is ironic that Lennon himself was unaware that everything he wishes to negate in the song were products of imagination. On a more serious note, the study of human imagination has received scant attention in the field of psychology, most probably because it is not amenable to simple measurement, and also possibly because of it has vague connections with the muses, unknowable external sources of thoughts and ideas.

Yet imagination is arguably more important to the ways humans think than so-called rational thinking, using logic and deductive reasoning described by psychologists as cognitive information processing, the kind of thinking associated with problem solving, IQ tests, and intelligence.

In its continuing claims to scientific respectability, academic psychology continues to hold onto a mechanistic scientism, concentrating on modelling brain processes which correspond to biology and physiology, shunning anything which cannot be observed and measured. Imagination, like other concepts such as mind, consciousness, soul, being immeasurable, might gain a brief mention, but are passed over quickly, unless they can in some way be translated into modern terminology. But occasionally, a new boy will put his head above the academic trench unaware that snipers are awaiting such boldness.

The new boys, brazenly combining evolutionary theories with any other academic disciplines which suites their purpose, are delighted to take the head-shots from the old-school snipers if it gives them further recognition, for Darwinian evolutionary theory has become most fashionable, eclipsing even Marxism and Existentialism.

So what we glean from this already rich source of ideas is that imagination is OK! And that 35, 000 years ago we humans discovered how to access the `dreaming brain` which permits us to utilise our memories and visualise possible futures, and consider abstract questions and possibilities. But the acid test of whether this actually happened is to check out its adaptive usefulness. The evolutionists main claim to the imagination`s evolutionary importance is that it would permit a kind of predictive thinking, useful for considering the range of possible outcomes during hunting! But if humans were interested only in survival it would seem that our newly found ability to imagine as a what-if facility is a very blunt cognitive tool. But understandingly, the new boys need to maintain their Darwinian beliefs intact, and any suggestion that imagination , as a significant evolutionary leap forward, might have given rise to anything remotely transcendent is anathema. But that is exactly what Maurice Bloch, an LSE anthropologist suggests in his idea of the` transcendental social`, a way of thinking about entities and beings that do not actually exist, and the ability to transcend both space and time beyond the physical and material limitations of our bodies. One manifestation of this new way of thinking was the emergence of religion, of visualising gods and an afterlife.

Understandably, the new boys are not comfortable with this idea, although some of them are happy to link it with distorted thinking associated with mental illness, and certainly they are aware that imagination is essential to creative thinking and ambiguity, and perhaps intuition, and in sensing something which is not physically present, which gets dangerously close to psychic phenomena!

To neuroscientists the imagination is a particular facility, one among many, which processes sense perceptions derived from our external environment which permits us to elaborate mental images created through what we see, hear, smell, etc. It is neither primary nor central to the cognitive process, for the modern view of how the brain works is that there is no coordinating or unifying centre, but that all thinking is a consequence of cognitive fluidity. Conventional psychology and evolutionary psychology also share this view, principally because to suggest otherwise would be to imply that there is within the human frame something which is uniquely and essentially individual, something we might claim to be a `self` or even worse, a `soul`. But Emanuel Kant identified imagination as central to our thinking and our sense of being. He claimed that, "Imagination is a blind and indispensible function of the soul, without which we should have no knowledge whatever, but of which we are scarcely even conscious". In other words, we just take our imagination for granted.

The evolutionary watershed that perhaps occurred 35, 000 years ago which led to being able to think beyond the immediate situation and which allowed us to visualise alternative futures, to empathise with others, and raise abstract questions and formulate satisfactory answers, also gave us the capacity to deal with despair, which surely is as essential to survival as being able to plan, and hunt, and avoid physical dangers. For the emergence of the imagination was a double edged adaptation, enabling us to reach out beyond ourselves, to empathise, to share our thoughts, to entertain others, to heal, to perform; but it also had a darker downside, the discovery of our own mortality. Surely the real adaptive value of the imagination was in dealing with the despair of our own deaths and the deaths of our loved ones.

If this led to the invention of religion it was surely via something much more abstract, through the idea of an essential and unique inner-self, which eventually we could understand as something invisible, beyond the immediate physical constraints of time and place, as Wordsworth would describe as, `the presence`, `a sense sublime`, `a motion and spirit that impels all thinking things, all objects of all thought`.

While dedicated evolutionists are in general agreement that the course of human evolution as more or less described by Darwin, they differ over the more subtle steps such as the emergence of consciousness, not that any of them are too clear what they mean by that term. And especially in the case of the discovery of the soul, which Peter Watson in his monumental history of Ideas, quoting the historian S.G.Brandon, describes as , "humanity`s most fundamental concept ", an idea which continues to haunt the modern mind.

But perhaps what is even more perplexing for the new boys, who are dedicated to the elimination of the idea of `soul`, is how they themselves deal with the sources of their own imagination and creativity. In their writings they occasionally let slip a hint of a remote belief in inspiration or their muse, an external presence, which as we all know refers to the possibility of something sublimely mystical that is better not mentioned!

Canto XXI

Eradicating The Word Soul

THE REMOVAL OF words such as aisle and chapel from the Oxford Junior Dictionary, because they had Christian connotations, has disturbed a small minority of individuals and created a minor flurry of protesting e-mails. Interestingly the word SOUL survives, but perhaps for not much longer. The removal of words from a dictionary, even a children's dictionary does not obliterate them from the language, or their significance from the culture, but it does perhaps signal a diminishing interest in an area of national or cultural activity.

But would it really matter if the word `soul` became redundant in a culture which objectivises and concretises every human activity to the extent that human beings are fast becoming characterised by their material possessions rather than what they think and feel. Its extinction would, in the main, be described simply as `going with the flow`, and not a matter for alarm. The word `soul` itself is used in popular journalism as a vague gap-filler where no modern equivalent word can express something ineffable or sublime. It catches my eye once or twice a week in newspapers as an enticement to readers that what follows will take them beyond the surface of things, but usually disappointingly a mere trick to ensnare the imagination.

But imagine some future event, similar to Chairman Mao's Cultural Revolution but massively on the grandest possible international scale, to enact a global Autos de fe in which the word SOUL suddenly became meaningless, not just allowed to fizzle out, but to be positively hounded to oblivion, and to be struck out of every document or artefact, paintings, music, literature, poems, in fact from anything with even the slenderest connection or reference to SOUL, to be destroyed so completely, that the next generation would be unable to gain the slightest hint that such an idea had ever existed. What would remain?

The images that come to mind are of empty wastelands, devoid of human life and with mounds of smoking ashes of burnt books and ideas! And suppose for a moment that the kind of madness that grips regimes and nations from time to time actually occurred in this era of technological control, commencing with an international celebration of book-burning circling the world with a ring of fire! And after the books, the demolition of buildings and monuments, and all of the worlds temples and sacred sites, the re-drawing of maps, the re-writing of history, the denial of memories, and so on and so forth, humanity and civilisation would shrink. But we know that it could never happen like this. Instead, the word will lose its coinage not through barbarism, but by gradual and flippant neglect.

The possible complete eradication of any concept as described above would surely be the ultimate litmus test of its value, and it would be difficult, almost impossible in fact, to imagine any other similar concept having quite the same effect as the loss of the concept SOUL. Without the idea of soul the gaps in western history would render it incomprehensible, perhaps more than ninety per cent of western philosophy would be struck out, the same with western music; Shakespeare in his entirety would disappear, the great art galleries would be empty.

Canto XXII

EVERY SEVENTEEN YEARS a particular species of cicada appears in Washington DC, apparently in their millions. They climb out of their holes, and for a few weeks they become the dominant subject of conversations and news stories, and become briefly the guiding metaphors of social commentators. Their seventeen years sojourn underground is invested by commentators with a profound significance, with their appearance and habits symbolising some of the most desirable characteristics of the people, and especially of the leaders, of the capital of the USA. To dally with any of these frolicsome stories is to enjoy a brief respite from the more unpleasantly chilling news which is the consequence of the activities of those leaders. And it is also part of the current style of their communication to make use of anything, natural or otherwise to further their message.

But in the light of events which witness America's actions and intentions to dominate the world, we should not wait for the cicadas, for there is a more appropriate insect capable of speaking for the men from Washington, and also for the people of the whole western world, and that is the burrowing wasp, the yellow-winged Sphex (Sphex flavipennis), which preys on crickets. The Sphex, has something of the bearing of a warrior queen about her, for she is equipped with an impressive weapon, a poisoned lancet which is used to paralyse her victims, which she does with all of the precision of a laser guided bomb. After ambushing a cricket and wrestling it onto its back, the Sphex mounts her victim, and carefully squeezes the cricket's sides until the neck is fully exposed, and then with remarkable accuracy, plunges the poisoned lancet into the cricket`s neck and then the abdomen. The paralysed victim is then manoeuvred into an underground chamber, still on its back, and placed neatly alongside other similar victims, and then a single Sphex egg is carefully deposited on the cricket`s breast, the tenderest spot, ready for the offspring's first meal. Fortunately the poison is sufficient to maintain paralysis for several weeks while the grub devours the cricket, eating its way into the entrails of the paralysed cricket's body, and out again, leaving what still appears to be a complete cricket, but which in fact is an empty shell.

The genius of Washington DC, as the world capital of materialism, is that while it pretends to imitate the innocent cicada, it mimics the glorious Sphex, by immobilising its prey, devouring its soft centre, and leaving something that resembles its original appearance, which is nothing more than a vacant shell stamped with the imprint of western values .And this is how we in the west have all become, characterised by our emptiness, nothing more than lumps of flesh, consuming voraciously and awaiting to be consumed in turn by the voracious Sphex.

Canto XXII

THE CONSEQUENCES OF the diminution of the soul are more severe than can be imagined in a single moment of reflection, for they cut into our self-image like the slow agonising death of a thousand cuts. Perhaps that is why we avoid thinking about it, and also perhaps this is why those who have attempted to delve into the pathology of dead souls have become mad. The most obvious consequence is that we are all condemned to the one dimensional material world of things, where existence is the only predicate, and where the distinction between ourselves and other species is a few percent of our genes. If this is true then why should we claim to be anything other than mere flesh

Canto XXIII

THINKING AND TALKING and writing about the soul is oblique rather than direct and linear. There seems to be something difficult and perplexing about it. Ideas and intuitive guesses about it seem to be similar to our experiences of another dimension, never directly in our field of vision, but always peripheral, as if we somehow are able to grasp something of its nebulous qualities when we turn our heads and glimpse a hint of something from the corner of our eye-view. Other writers who have inadvertently found themselves heading in the same direction of soul-searching either pull back or are pulled into a vortex of ideas which are difficult to disentangle; but always there is the feeling of a `presence`.

In the poem `Tintern Abbey` William Wordsworth tells us that he feels a disturbing presence...that impels....and rolls through all things, and hearing `the still, sad music of humanity` he enters an unknown dimension beyond the reach of the majority of present-day individuals. Even in his own day, he knew that the possibility of these sublime feelings in others was being extinguished by the new urban culture, and in this sense his poetry assumes an unrecognised prophetic quality which resonates with the same purposeful energy of early Greek tragedians.

Although we cannot recreate the experiences of past generations, we know that poets of that era were regarded as teachers and prophets who could summon together, through their words, the collective souls of their audiences and also those of their ancestors. In fact this was the main purpose of the Chorus, especially in the Tragedies in which the main purpose was to help audiences to come to terms with their deepest thoughts of death, particularly their own, and consequently how to live their lives to the full. It was for this purpose that the grand entrance of the chorus had the effect of stunning the audience into silence and reverence, sometimes hypnotically confronting them with the presence of their own souls.

It is almost impossible for us to imagine the impact of this collective confrontation of psyche on an entire audience, for it goes beyond anything remotely comparably recognisable to modern minds, but it is for us, our loss of a sense of presence on that scale which underscores our deepest resentment with ourselves as the source of our alienation. To be aware of ourselves in this way would be to become sensitively responsive to both the physical and spiritual dimensions of existence in a way Wordsworth suggests.

Not only would we have we lost our sense of personal completeness, we would have diminished our familial and communal links, and forgotten our ancestors; even our previous generation would have all but disappeared! We would also have lost the language to express our regret; our poets too would have deserted us. The music finally would have stopped

Manufactured By: RR Donnelley
Breinigsville, PA USA
July, 2010